Knight's Cross, Oak Leaves and Swords Recipients 1941–45

Gordon Williamson · Illustrated by Ramiro Bujeiro

Consultant editor Martin Windrow

First published in Great Britain in 2005 by Osprey Publishing,
Midland House, West Way, Botley, Oxford, OX2 0PH, UK
443 Park Avenue South, New York, NY 10016, USA
Email: info@ospreypublishing.com

ISBN 1 84176 643 7

Page layout: Ken Vail Graphic Design, Cambridge, UK
Index by Alan Thatcher
Originated by PPS Grasmere, Leeds, UK
Printed in China through World Print Ltd.

05 06 07 08 09   10 9 8 7 6 5 4 3 2 1

A CIP catalogue record for this book is available from the British Library

FOR A CATALOGUE OF ALL BOOKS PUBLISHED BY OSPREY MILITARY
AND AVIATION PLEASE CONTACT:

North America:
Osprey Direct
2427 Bond Street, University Park, IL 60466, USA
Email: info@ospreydirectusa.com

All other regions:
Osprey Direct UK
PO Box 140, Wellingborough, Northants, NN8 2FA, UK
Email: info@ospreydirect.co.uk

Buy online at **www.ospreypublishing.com**

Author's Note

The rank under which each recipient is listed is that held at
the time of the award of the Swords.

Photographic credit

Unless otherwise indicated, all images are from the author's
collection.

Artist's Note

Readers may care to note that the original paintings from
which the colour plates in this book were prepared are
available for private sale. All reproduction copyright
whatsoever is retained by the Publishers. All enquiries
should be addressed to:

*Ramiro Bujeiro,
C.C.28,
1602 Florida
Argentina*

The Publishers regret that they can enter into no
correspondence upon this matter.

KNIGHT'S CROSS AND OAK-LEAVES WITH SWORDS RECIPIENTS 1941–45

INTRODUCTION

The re-institution, at the outbreak of World War II in September 1939, of the series of awards constituting the Order of the Iron Cross included as the senior award the Knight's Cross (*Ritterkreuz*). This could be awarded to any rank in the armed forces, either for individual or cumulative acts of gallantry or for distinguished leadership in command. After the first nine months of the war it was decided that additional grades were required, to further distinguish those who were already 'bearers' of the Knight's Cross (*Ritterkreuzträger*) and who continued to demonstrate exemplary courage on the battlefield or success in command. On 3 June 1940, Hitler signed a decree introducing the Oak-Leaves clasp (*Eichenlaub*); and on 21 June 1941, the Oak-Leaves with Swords (*Eichenlaub mit Schwerten*), for award to those who merited further distinction after previously being decorated with the Oak-Leaves. Like an oak-leaf spray, the swords were a traditional German device in use since Imperial times to indicate a higher grade of an order.[1]

Description

The Oak-Leaves with Swords clasp consisted of a set of die-struck oak-leaves to the base of which were soldered a pair of crossed swords, the latter usually being finely cast rather than die-struck. On the reverse was the typical 'paperclip'-style ribbon suspension loop, but – at least in the case of the official awards made by J.Godet und Sohn of Berlin – this loop was significantly longer than that used on the Oak-Leaves alone, to prevent the sword hilts from snagging on the top edge of the Knight's Cross.

Godet were the only firm contracted to manufacture this award for the Präsidialkanzlei, and the Oak-Leaves used were absolutely standard pieces, of both first and second types (as described and illustrated in Elite 123). As with the Oak-Leaves, the retail sale of this award was prohibited in mid 1941, but some examples made for the retail market before this prohibition do exist – e.g. those by Steinhauer und Lück of Lüdenscheid. On official award pieces the Swords featured detailing on both sides, though not on the examples made by Steinhauer und Lück.

The award was made from 900 grade silver (i.e. 900/1,000 parts pure silver), and was marked on the reverse exactly as were the Oak-Leaves: with the designation '900' on the left; and on the right either Godet's *Herstellermarke* 'L/50' – the retailer code allotted by the Association of German Orders Manufacturers (LDO) – together with the word 'SiLBER' in upper/lower case format, or the Präsidialkanzlei contract code '21'. Typically the overall dimensions of the clasp will be 27.1mm × 24.6mm.

---

[1] See the first two titles in this sequence: Elite 114, *Knight's Cross and Oak-Leaves Recipients 1939–40*; and Elite 123, *Knight's Cross and Oak-Leaves Recipients 1941–45*

The piece was presented in a small black leatherette-covered case typically measuring 104mm × 78mm × 23mm. A slot for the suspension loop allowed the clasp to sit flush against the black velvet covering the base; and a recess was provided above for a folded length of 45mm-wide neck ribbon. The lid was lined in white satin.

The clasp made by Steinhauer u.Lück featured much larger swords and has overall dimensions of 28mm × 30.5mm; it bore no contract code. Though somewhat unusual in appearance compared to the official award piece, Steinhauer u.Lück's wartime product has been positively identified from its distinctive Swords in an Imperial War Museum photograph of British servicemen posing with captured German awards in 1945. Other commercial pieces were manufactured by C.E.Juncker and Paul Meybauer, both of Berlin, these carrying the LDO codes 'L/12' and 'L/13' respectively.

These latter manufacturers' production runs were short, as the retail sale of this and other high grade awards was prohibited very shortly after the introduction of the Swords. Commercial stocks were ordered to be surrendered to the Präsidialkanzlei for addition to official stocks. Due to the extremely short period during which they were made, commercial examples by these three firms are not often encountered.

Although wartime jeweller-made copies and 'field-made' examples are both known, those not conforming to pieces made by the manufacturers noted above will generally not have anywhere near the value of a true award piece or legitimate commercial piece. It is difficult

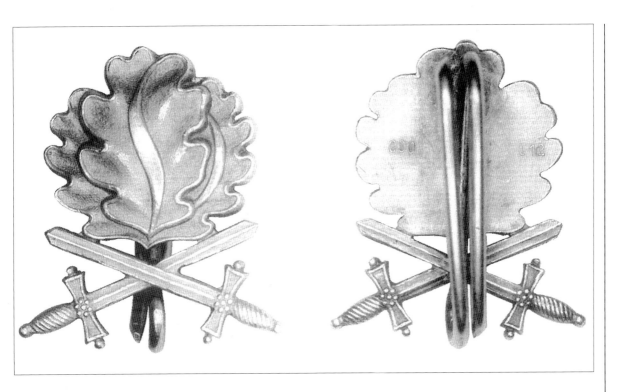

ABOVE Oak-Leaves with Swords clasp by the renowned Berlin firm of C.E.Juncker. Close comparison with the formal award piece made by Godet (Plate A2) reveals a number of subtle differences in the characteristics of the Oak-Leaves. As Juncker were never given an official contract to supply the decoration, this piece simply bears their retailer code 'L/12'. The silver is of 800 grade rather than the 900 used by Godet. (Detlev Niemann)

LEFT The award of the Oak-Leaves with Swords generally took place at a special ceremony at the Führerhauptquartier; photographers were usually on hand to record the event for posterity, as here for the award to the Crimea hero Maj Erich Bärenfänger. On many occasions groups received their decorations at the same time; more 'important' recipients would be granted a personal audience with Hitler. (US National Archives)

to overstate the extreme rarity of original examples of this award, which at the time of writing are attracting sterling prices well into five figures. It should also be noted that this award has been heavily faked for many years, in qualities ranging from crude to nearly perfect.

When a whole range of wartime decorations were authorized for wear once again in new 'de-Nazified' forms following the Ordens Gesetz

The cover of the folder for the Oak-Leaves with Swords document. The workmanship and detail of the gilt national emblem and the intricate geometric border are of the highest quality. (Detlev Niemann)

of 1957, Steinhauer u.Lück began producing Oak-Leaves with Swords once again. Early pieces were very well made, but as time went on quality deteriorated drastically, and most later pieces were made in brass with a poor quality silver plating. Even the solid silver pieces (more recent examples being in 925 grade) have poor definition and are not as well finished as originals. Although still considered as an officially approved decoration, these later pieces are generally treated as being made for the collector market and are of low value.

Documents

When the Swords were awarded, the recipient was given a small A5-size pre-printed document, the Vorläufiges Besitzzeugnis or 'Preliminary Certificate' of possession. This had his personal details typewritten into the appropriate spaces, was signed by the awarding authority at bottom right, and bore an ink-stamped seal in the lower left corner.

At some later date, a magnificent formal award document or Urkunde was presented. This was made from parchment, consisting of a large sheet folded in half to give the effect of four A3-size sheets. On what would be page 3 the details of the award were hand-lettered in exquisite calligraphy and tooled in gold leaf. At the top was the national eagle-and-swastika emblem with outstretched wings, in gold. This was followed by the text *Im Namen/ des Deutschen Volkes/ verleihe ich dem* [rank, name hand-tooled in gold leaf] *das Echenlaub/ mit Schwertern/ zum Ritterkreuz/ des Eisernen Kreuzes.* Then followed *Berlin, dem* [date of award]. Just below this was added the signature of Adolf Hitler, usually in genuine manuscript rather than facsimile.

This document was contained in a superb folder or Mappe, made from board covered with white leather and with inside covers lined in parchment. A large gilt folded-wing national emblem adorned the face of the folder, which was bordered with a geometric design in gilt metal. In the centre a narrow ribbon held the folded Urkunde in place. The lower edge of the rear inner face of the folder bore the name of the craftswoman Frieda Thiersch.

Unlike the award itself, which was made up in small batches by the manufacturer, with an over-capacity resulting in numbers of unawarded examples still being in storage at the end of the war, the Urkunden were made strictly to order – a time-consuming process for skilled hands. Being unique, and named to an individual whose career is well documented, they are therefore far rarer than original examples of the award itself and command commensurately high prices.

Distribution

The distribution of awards of the Swords clasp, by date and service, shows some interesting trends.

The bulk of the initial awards were to Luftwaffe fighter aces, with a handful to the most successful U-boat commanders – in other words, all

	Army	Luftwaffe	Navy	SS	
1941	0	4	1	0	
1942	3	13	2	0	
1943	10	6	1	2	
1944	40	22	1	13	
1945	25	7	0	9	
Totals:	78	52	5	24	(159)

were to men whose achievements could be quantified, in number or tonnage of 'kills'. No Army or Waffen-SS soldiers received the award in 1941 despite the massive extension of the ground war by the invasion of the USSR that June; the Oak-Leaves were apparently sufficient to recognize distinguished gallantry or command success. Even in 1942 the Luftwaffe again predominated, its pilots achieving unprecedented numbers of aerial victories over the large but poorly equipped and trained Red Air Force. But as the equipment and skill of their opponents improved, and the victories required to obtain the Swords became harder to achieve, so Luftwaffe awards declined. Similarly, as Army troops became involved in bitter defensive actions as well as offensives, so awards to the Army increased, and defeat in North Africa soon led to another front opening up in Italy. Navy awards remained

Hitler admires the craftsmanship of the folder or *Mappe* containing the formal *Urkunde* for the Oak-Leaves with Swords. This gives a good impression of the size and bulk of this item. (US National Archives)

constant at one or two per year; despite the larger numbers of U-boats on patrol, May 1943 saw the Allies definitively seizing the advantage in the Battle of the Atlantic, and submarine losses increased sharply.

By 1944 the Luftwaffe was outnumbered on all fronts, and suffering serious losses among irreplaceable experienced aircrew; while some of the leading aces continued to build extraordinary scores, proportionately Luftwaffe awards declined as compared to those of the ground forces. The Army and Waffen-SS were now on the retreat on the Eastern Front and, with the Allied landings in Normandy, were forced to fight a war on three fronts simultaneously. In 1945 the Luftwaffe was a spent force, and Army and Waffen-SS awards numbered almost five times as many as those to aircrew. By 1944 the Battle of the Atlantic was lost, and the U-boat captains faced a constant struggle simply to survive, let alone to achieve any major successes against enemy shipping.

By far the greatest number of awards of the Swords related to the monumental struggle between the Wehrmacht and the Red Army on the Russian Front; and this title is therefore devoted predominantly to a selection of those who fought in the East.

SS-Ostubaf Günther Eberhard Wisliceny wearing the Knight's Cross with Oak-Leaves and Swords, as commander of the 'Deutschland' Regt of 2.SS-Pz Div 'Das Reich' during the final battles in Hungary and Austria. He was officially awarded the Swords only on 6 May 1945, two days before the end of the war, and was decorated at the front by the C-in-C 6.SS-Panzerarmee, SS-Obstgruf 'Sepp' Dietrich. In some cases of these very late awards, photographs of them being worn are evidently retouched, since there was no opportunity for the recipient to pose for a portrait.

KNIGHT'S CROSS WITH OAK-LEAVES AND SWORDS RECIPIENTS

Hauptmann Hans Philipp

Hans Philipp was born on 17 March 1917 at Meissen. On completion of his flying training and being commissioned Leutnant he was posted to fly Messerschmitt Bf 109E fighters. Serving with I Gruppe of Jagdgeschwader 26 'Schlageter', he saw combat in September 1939 over Poland, where on the 5th he shot down his first enemy aircraft, a PZL 24. During the 1940 campaign in the West, Oberleutnant Philipp flew as the Staffelkapitän (squadron leader), leading the eight other pilots of 4 Staffel, II Gruppe of the new JG 54. The new Geschwader took as their emblem a large green heart painted below their cockpits, and Philipp and his comrades were nicknamed the *Grünherzjäger*. During the Battle of Britain he quickly gained a reputation as a skilled 'dog-fighter'; 20 October 1940 brought Philipp his 20th victory, and the award of the Knight's Cross followed two days later. He was only the second pilot in JG 54 to receive this decoration.

On 5 April 1941, Hitler launched his troops into the troublesome Balkans as a necessary but time-wasting prelude to his planned invasion of Russia. Two days later JG 54 was in action against Yugoslav pilots, who were also flying Bf 109s purchased during a period of more friendly relations. When the Yugoslavs attacked Ju 87 Stuka dive-bombers which were being escorted by JG 54, Philipp succeeded in downing two of the enemy Messerschmitts.

It was after the opening of Operation 'Barbarossa' in June, however, that Philipp's score began to mount rapidly. He was awarded the Oak-Leaves on 24 August 1941. When the Gruppenkommandeur of I/JG 54, Franz Eckerle, was reported missing in action on 14 February 1942, Hans Philipp was appointed as his replacement. In his new role as group commander, with 30 pilots looking to him for leadership, he oversaw the early careers of several young Jagdflieger who would later come to prominence, among them Walter Nowotny. On 12 March 1942, Philipp became the first member of JG 54 to receive the Swords, and only the eighth recipient of this decoration; and on 31 March he was only the fourth fighter pilot ever to achieve 100 aerial victories. Just under a year later he was the second to record 200 kills.

April 1943 saw the now Major Philipp transferred to the West and, at the age of only 26, to command of 100-odd fighters as Geschwader Kommodore of JG 1 'Oesau'. The daylight raids by the heavy bombers of the US 8th Army Air Force were increasing, and JG 1 were employed on Reichsverteidigung (home defence) duties over the Dutch coast with a mixture of Bf 109Gs and Fw 190As. Philipp brought a touch of Russian Front rigour to JG 1, which he believed had been getting a little too used to the comforts of a Western European posting. His command responsibilities kept him on the ground more than he liked, during a summer of increasingly intense daylight battles.

Although JG 1 played its part in the great Luftwaffe victory of 17 August 1943, when the 8th AAF lost 60 Flying Fortresses during the Schweinfurt/Regensburg raids, the appearance that month of long-range P-47 escorts with belly-tanks changed the whole balance of the fighting. Reichs-marschall Göring refused to accept this, however, and berated his fighter pilots for incompetence and actual cowardice. After a raid on Frankfurt on 4 October he issued furious orders that (a) there were no weather conditions bad enough to prevent interceptors from taking off; (b) any pilot who returned from a mission in an undamaged aircraft without having scored a kill would be court-martialled; and (c) that a pilot who had used up his ammunition, or whose guns had jammed, was to ram an enemy bomber. Such petulant ranting earned the contempt of veteran combat officers, and Philipp simply declared that he would ignore it.

Oberleutnant Hans Philipp, shown here just after the award of the Oak-Leaves. At this point he had just become only the eighth recipient of the award, and a few days later would become the fourth German fighter pilot to exceed 100 aerial victories.

The distinctive 'crazy paving' camouflage scheme identifies these yellow-nosed Bf 109Es as belonging to II/JG 54, with which Philipp flew in the early weeks of the Russian campaign when he won his Oak-Leaves. By June 1941 most Jagdgruppen in the East had already received the superior Bf 109F model. (Hans Obert Collection)

On 8 October 1943 the USAAF sent over 150 bombers with 250 fighter escorts to hit shipyards in north Germany engaged in the production of U-boats. JG 1 was scrambled, and a dog-fight with the escorts ensued. Over the radio Oberstleutnant Philipp was heard claiming his first heavy bomber shot down, and instructing his wingman to follow him into another attack. That was the last that was heard from him; his wingman saw Philipp's aircraft disappear into cloud, and later that day the news was received that he had been shot down and killed by P-47s. Hans Philipp had flown over 500 sorties and scored a total of 206 victories.

Oberleutnant Max-Hellmuth Ostermann

Born in Hamburg on 11 December 1917, Max-Hellmuth Ostermann joined the Luftwaffe in March 1937 as an officer candidate. On completion of his training and a commission as Leutnant he was posted to Zerstörer Geschwader 1, flying the twin-engined Messerschmitt Bf 110 heavy fighter. He saw service with I/ZG 1 during the campaign in Poland, where the Bf 110 was a match for most of the Polish aircraft it would encounter. This would be far from the case in later campaigns, however, and Ostermann was fortunate to be transferred to what was then JG 21 to fly the far superior single-engined Bf 109; the Bf 110 squadrons would suffer serious losses at the hands of the faster and more manoeuvrable RAF Hurricanes and Spitfires during the Battle of Britain.

On 20 May 1940, Ostermann scored his first aerial victory when he shot down a French Morane 406 over Peronne. Six days later a second French fighter fell to his guns, a Curtiss Hawk encountered near Arras. On 6 June, JG 21 was redesignated JG 54. It would be another two months before Ostermann added to his score, by shooting down a

Spitfire on the morning of 12 August. A second Spitfire followed at the end of that month, and on 5 September Ostermann brought his score to five with a victory over a Hurricane. Before the end of the Battle of Britain he had raised his total tally to eight aerial victories.

In the spring of 1941 he was in action over the Balkans where – like Hans Philipp – he came up against Yugoslav Air Force Messerschmitt Bf 109Es, shooting one down over Belgrade on 6 April. It was in the opening stages of the invasion of the Soviet Union in June that Ostermann's score began to accelerate. Flying over the Leningrad front, his shot down his first two Soviet aircraft on 23 June 1941, and by the end of July his tally had passed 20 kills. On 14 September, with his score standing at 30, he was awarded the Knight's Cross. He continued to stack up victories – 50 by early in 1942, including US Lend-Lease types such as a C-47 Dakota transport and P-40 fighters. By now promoted Oberleutnant, Ostermann was appointed Staffelkapitän of 8/JG 54 in February 1942; and on 12 March, with 60 kills to his name, he was decorated with the Oak-Leaves. Before the end of that month he would achieve yet another 20 victories.

On 10 May 1942, Ostermann shot down his 97th enemy aircraft, an Ilyushin 180, but was himself shot down only minutes afterwards. He returned to his unit safely; two days later he took his revenge, shooting down an I-16 and two Curtiss P-40s to make him only the seventh pilot to achieve 100 aerial victories, though in the process his own Bf 109F-4 was hit and he was wounded. Just five days later Ostermann was awarded the Swords in recognition of his hundredth kill, and sent for a spell of home leave.

ABOVE LEFT **Hans Philipp as a Hauptmann, apparently showing him wearing the Oak-Leaves with Swords. In fact this photo has had the Swords touched in by an artist; this was common practice even before the last days of the war, by the firms who produced such propaganda postcards for sale.**

ABOVE RIGHT **Oberleutnant Max-Hellmuth Ostermann as Staffelkapitän of 8/JG 54 in a portrait taken after the Swords were awarded following his hundredth aerial victory. He is wearing the official Godet-made presentation set.**

Oberleutnant Max-Hellmuth Ostermann receives the Oak-Leaves from Hitler at a ceremony at the *Wolfsschanze* in spring 1942. At this point his score stood at over 60 kills.

Bf 110Bs of I/ZG 1 over Poland, September 1939. Ostermann's Gruppe achieved a total of six 'kills' in Poland, but lost two of its three Staffelkapitane to PZL P. 11 fighters. He was probably fortunate to transfer to a Bf 109 unit before the Battle of Britain.

Ostermann returned to the 'Green Hearts' in August 1942, adding another victory on the 8th of that month. Late in the morning of 9 August, in a dog-fight over Amossovo, he claimed his 102nd and final victory, but was himself shot down and killed. By the time of his death Ostermann had flown over 300 combat missions.

Oberfeldwebel Leopold Steinbatz

Leopold Steinbatz, born in Vienna on 25 October 1918, enlisted in the Austrian Army in 1937. After the Anschluss with Germany the following year he found himself a member of the Wehrmacht, and in 1939 transferred to the Luftwaffe, where he was accepted for flying training. Steinbatz joined 9 Staffel, III Gruppe of the fighter wing JG 52 as an NCO pilot, flying the Messerschmitt Bf 109E. Too late to see action in the 1940 campaigns, he gained valuable combat experience during the brief operations over the Balkans the following spring, and in the attack on Crete where, principally on ground attack missions, he flew alongside the future leading ace Hermann Graf.

Steinbatz was not to open his own score until the opening stages of the invasion of the USSR in summer 1941, but once let loose in that extraordinarily 'target-rich' environment the young sergeant revealed a remarkable natural talent for aerial combat. On 1 August he shot down his first enemy aircraft, and by the end of November his tally had mounted to 25 kills, bringing him the award of the Luftwaffe Goblet of Honour on 8 December. On 22 January 1942 he was awarded the German Cross in Gold; and only three weeks later, on 14 February 1942, Feldwebel Steinbatz was decorated with the Ritterkreuz after reaching a score of 42 victories. Shortly afterwards he was promoted to Oberfeldwebel. On 5 May 'Bazi' Steinbatz shot down his 50th enemy aircraft; three days later he destroyed no fewer than seven Soviet aircraft; by 20 May his score had reached 75; and on 2 June, having increased his total to 90 aerial victories, this extraordinary month of success was crowned by the award of the Oak-Leaves.

There appeared to be no stopping Steinbatz, and by 15 June 1942 he had been credited with 99 victories; but then, while returning from a combat sortie, his Bf 109F was hit by a lucky shot from enemy flak. Unable to bale out, he was killed when it crashed into a forest near Voltschansk. Steinbatz was posthumously awarded the Swords and commissioned Leutnant. In a combat career of less than two years he had flown more than 300 combat sorties; had he survived longer, there is little doubt that his skills as a pilot and marksman would have taken him into the ranks of the Luftwaffe's highest scoring aces.

Oberstleutnant Wolf-Dietrich Wilcke

This officer's early career as a fighter pilot was a good deal more eventful than that of Steinbatz, but led on to even greater success, senior command, and renown throughout his service. Born at Schrimm, Posen, on 11 March 1913, Wilcke enlisted in the cavalry in 1934 before transferring to the newly revealed Luftwaffe the following year as an officer candidate, and after completing training he was posted to Jagdgeschwader 132. He had shown great natural talent, and spent about 18 months as a flying instructor at the Jagdfliegerschule at Werneuchen before being selected to go to Spain with the Condor Legion. After a brief and relatively uneventful spell of duty there he returned to Germany and joined II/JG 53. By the outbreak of war he had reached the rank of Hauptmann and was appointed Staffelkapitän of 7/JG 53 in the 'Ace of Spades' Geschwader's new III Gruppe.

His successes in aerial combat began when he shot down a French Potez 637 over the Saar valley on 7 November 1939. His career might have come to a premature end on 18 May 1940, when he was bounced by French Curtiss Hawk 75 fighters after becoming separated from the rest of his squadron, and his Bf 109E was shot down. He was taken prisoner, but following the successful conclusion of the campaign against France he was quickly released to rejoin his unit. On 13 August, during the Battle of Britain, his aircraft developed engine trouble and he was forced to bale out over the Channel, but he was spotted by a Dornier Do 18 rescue seaplane. By the end of this eventful spell of duty Wilcke had scored 13 aerial victories.

During the summer of 1941, Wilcke commanded III/JG 53 in the opening phases of Operation 'Barbarossa'. On the first day of the campaign on the northern sector, Wilcke and his squadron were returning from their first combat sortie against Soviet airfields in Lithuania when they encountered a number of obsolete I-15 biplanes. Wilcke succeeded in shooting down three, and another two victories later that day raised his total to 18 enemy aircraft destroyed. Yet another close brush with disaster quickly followed, however: on 25 June a collision with another fighter during take-off caused both aircraft to burst into flames, but Wilcke's luck held up and he escaped with only minor injuries. On 6 August 1941, credited with 25 enemy aircraft destroyed, Hauptmann Wilcke received the Knight's Cross.

ABOVE **Oberstleutnant Wolf-Dietrich Wilcke, Geschwaderkommodore of JG 3 'Udet'. At the time of his Swords award in December 1942, Wilcke's Geschwader was providing all fighter support for the 6.Armee trapped at Stalingrad. He would die 15 months later while flying against US 8th AF heavy bombers over Germany. Wilcke was regarded with great respect and affection throughout the Jagdwaffe, and was nicknamed 'Fürst' – 'the Prince'.**

LEFT **On a Russian airstrip in late summer 1941, Wilcke (centre) enjoys a smoke with two other Ritterkreuzträger of his Gruppe, III/JG 53: Lts Herbert Schramm (left) and Erich Schmidt.**

In December 1941, by which time his score had risen to 32, Wilcke's Gruppe was transferred to Sicily. During sorties over the island of Malta, Wilcke added four Spitfires to his tally. From Sicily, III/JG 53 were sent to North Africa in May 1942; but Wilcke received transfer orders, to join JG 3 'Udet' on the Russian Front. Three months later Major Wilcke was appointed Kommodore of JG 3. His score continued to rise at an impressive rate, and during the push to the Volga in summer 1942 he brought his tally to 100 victories by 6 September. This achievement brought him the Oak-Leaves to his Knight's Cross three days later; and during the month of September alone, he added more than 30 further victories to his log-book.

Wilcke's staff controlled all fighter operations in the battle for Stalingrad, with aircraft operating at first from that city's Pitomnik airfield. As the situation on the ground deteriorated the pilots shifted from flying offensive sorties to providing escort cover for transport aircraft bringing in supplies. On 17 December alone Wilcke made five further kills, bringing his total to 151. He was only the fourth pilot to record this achievement, which brought him the Swords on 23 December 1942 (by which date his score had actually reached 155). With the end in sight at Stalingrad, however, JG 3 were forced to pull out to avoid being trapped in the 'pocket'. Based at Tazinskaya from early January 1943, JG 3 continued to fly support missions to Stalingrad until the Sixth Army finally surrendered. JG 3 subsequently fought over the Kuban bridgehead as the Soviets continued their push westwards. However, the award of the Swords to fighter pilots in senior command positions brought automatic grounding; the risk of losing a leader of such experience and capabilities was considered too high.

In spring 1943, the Staff flight and I/JG 3 were moved back to Germany to join the Reichsverteidigung home defence command, as the USAAF day bombing campaign over occupied Western Europe began to

The battle by the Reichsverteidigung wings – like Wilcke's JG 3 – against the formations of American four-engined day bombers involved not only the routine fitting of 30mm cannon in 'gondolas' beneath the wings of the Bf 109G-6, but also experiments with these 2cm rocket launchers (here on aircraft of an unidentified squadron), and even air-dropped bombs. Pilots had varying success with these expedients, but in 1944 the certainty of encountering long-range P-51 Mustang escort fighters meant that they had to be abandoned; they made the Bf 109 and Fw 190 too unwieldly to protect themselves in a dog-fight. (Franz Selinger Collection)

reach into Germany itself. Early in August the rest of the Geschwader joined them, based initially at Mönchengladbach; II Gruppe were tasked with flying top cover against the increasingly numerous and dangerous US fighter escorts, while the Bf 109G-6 'gunboats' of I and III/JG 3 hit the heavy bombers. Oberstleutnant Wilcke grew increasingly frustrated at being grounded, and after obeying the order for about a year he eventually began ignoring it. During February 1944 he downed four B-17 Flying Fortresses – an extremely hazardous feat, for which fighter pilots gained much respect. On 6 March, Wilcke's Bf 109G-6 was badly shot up during a dog-fight with US fighters and he was forced to crash-land near Neuruppin, but again, he escaped any major injury.

On 23 March 1944, as he led his Geschwader in an attack on a large US bomber formation near Braunschweig, he came to the aid of his wingman and shot down a P-51 – his 162nd victory. Shortly afterwards Oberst Wolf-Dietrich Wilcke was shot down and killed by two other Mustangs of the US 336th Fighter Squadron. The 31-year-old colonel had flown more than 730 combat missions.

Generalmajor Karl Eibl

Karl Eibl began his military career with the Imperial Austrian Army at the outbreak of World War I. Commissioned Leutnant in Landwehr Regt 21, he was promoted to Oberleutnant in 1915. After the war Eibl remained in the military, gaining promotion to Hauptmann and eventually being posted to Inf Regt 6 of the Austrian Army. Following the Anschluss with Germany in 1938 he was taken into the Wehrmacht, and by 1939 held the rank of Oberstleutnant and command of Inf Regt 131, part of 44.Infanterie Division. During the Polish campaign his skilled leadership earned him both classes of the Iron Cross.

During the 1940 campaign against France and the Low Countries, Eibl commanded the sister regiment, Inf Regt 132, in the same division. For the defeat of a French brigade and the seizure of strategically important territory around Chuignolles, he was decorated with the Knight's Cross on 15 August 1940. After the Westfeldzug, Eibl remained in France on occupation duties until his regiment was moved to the Balkans in preparation for Operation 'Barbarossa'. At the head of Inf Regt 132, Oberst Eibl saw intense fighting around Zhitomir and in the Zwiahel bridgehead close to the Uman peninsula; successful command in these actions brought him the Oak-Leaves on 31 December 1941, followed two months later by promotion to Generalmajor and command of 385.Infanterie Division.

Eibl's new command was involved in heavy fighting on the Don river front in winter 1942; during the Soviet counter-offensive following the encirclement of 6.Armee at Stalingrad the division succeded in halting the enemy advance in its sector north of the city, and for this achievement GenMaj Eibl received the Swords on 19 December 1942, as only the second Army officer awarded this decoration (the first being Erwin Rommel). On 1 January 1943, Eibl was promoted to Generalleutnant and handed over his division, still embroiled in bitter fighting, when he moved to take command of XXIV Panzerkorps. As part of 4.Panzerarmee this corps was tasked with attempting to break the Soviet encirclement; after making slow but steady progress this break-through attempt was finally halted just 30 miles from the Stalingrad perimeter.

Karl Eibl is seen here as an Oberstleutnant, commanding Infanterie Regiment 132, during the award ceremony for his Knight's Cross in France in August 1940; most often the presentation was made 'in the field'.

A fresh Soviet armoured advance in the Voronezh sector outflanked XXIV Panzerkorps as well as Italian Alpini units. Eibl barely managed to save his corps during a desperate break-out through enemy lines to the west; but in confused fighting in foggy conditions Eibl's headquarters column ran into an Italian unit who mistook the Germans for Soviet troops. During a panicky exchange of fire a grenade landed near Eibl, causing serious leg wounds and heavy loss of blood. At a field hospital surgeons were forced to carry out an emergency amputation; GenLt Eibl survived the operation, but died a few hours later. Karl Eibl was posthumously promoted to General der Infanterie on 1 March 1943.

Generaloberst Hermann Hoth

Hermann Hoth was born in Neuruppin on 12 April 1885, the son of an army medical officer. He joined the Army as an officer cadet in 1904, and made good progress; by 1914 he was already a Hauptmann serving with the General Staff. During World War I he served in a number of units, and at one point commanded a Fliegerabteilung. By the end of the war he was a Generalstabsoffizier with an infantry division. In the post-war Reichsheer he progressed through various staff and command appointments; by the formation of the new Wehrmacht in 1935 he was leading 18.Inf Div as a Generalmajor. In 1938 he was promoted Generalleutnant and given command of XV Armeekorps.

His command was up-graded to XV Panzerkorps the following year, and he led it with conspicuous success during the invasion of Poland in September 1939. Hoth was among the officers decorated with the first examples of the newly created Knight's Cross, the award being bestowed on 27 October 1939. The Western campaign in spring 1940 saw Hoth given command of 10.Armee; once again successes came swiftly, and Hoth was promoted to full General on 19 July 1940.

For the invasion of the USSR in June 1941, Hoth was given command of Panzergruppe 3, which made highly successful thrusts deep into Soviet territory, capturing Minsk and Vitebsk and taking vast numbers of prisoners before turning towards Moscow. On 17 July 1941, Gen Hoth was awarded the Oak-Leaves. In October he was transferred to the southern sector of the front, where he would serve as commander-in-chief (Oberbefehlshaber) of 17.Armee with the rank of Generaloberst. Hoth led 17.Armee through many battles around Kharkov and in the Donets basin as the Soviets launched their counter-offensive in January 1942. In the summer of 1942 he took over from GenObst Höpner as commander of 4.Panzerarmee, fighting on the Voronezh front; and in December his army took part in the abortive attempt to relieve the encircled 6.Armee at Stalingrad. Nevertheless, in February/March 1943 Hoth won a crushing victory in the third battle of Kharkov.

In July 1943, GenObst Hoth's army formed the armoured spearhead of GFM von Manstein's Heeresgruppe Sud, the southern pincer of Hitler's massive and ill-fated offensive against the Soviet forces in the Kursk salient. For this Operation 'Citadel', Hoth commanded II SS-Panzer Korps (divisions 'Leibstandarte', 'Das Reich' & 'Totenkopf'); XLVIII Panzerkorps (3rd & 11th PzDivs, PzGren Div 'Grossdeutschland' & 167th Inf Div); and LII Armeekorps (57th, 255th & 332nd Inf Divs), with air support from the whole of Luftflotte 4. When his 700 tanks (including about 60 of the new heavy PzKw VI Tigers) were unleashed on 5 July, Hoth made rapid progress, inflicting huge casualties on LtGen Chistyakov's 6th Guard Army. But the enormous depth of the Soviet defences, prepared in anticipation of the German attacks, soaked up Hoth's troops and tanks at a terrifying rate – and the Red Army could replace these losses a great deal more easily than the Wehrmacht. When they launched their own long-planned Operation 'Kutuzov' against the Orel Bulge to the north of the salient on 12 July, the German operations around Orel and Kursk were doomed. Hitler was unnerved by the simultaneous Allied

A formal study of Generaloberst Hermann Hoth taken just after the presentation of the Swords, when he was C-in-C (Oberbefehlshaber) of 4.Panzerarmee. Hitler dismissed Hoth – one of his most successful Panzer generals – from active command at the end of 1943, largely as a scapegoat for the results of the Führer's own disastrous meddling; he called Hoth 'a bird of ill-omen... a defeatist'. Hoth's was one of a number of cases in which commanders who had fallen out of favour were awarded an important decoration at the same time as being relieved of their commands.

invasion of Sicily, and withdrew some of Hoth's best units. During the Soviet counter-offensive of July–August the Red Army broke through and recaptured Kharkov. On 15 September 1943, Hoth was awarded the Swords; but in November the Red Army recaptured Kiev, a setback which infuriated Hitler. Hoth was sent on leave, and on 10 December 1943 he was relieved of his command, recalled to Germany and placed on the reserve; he was never given another combat command. After the war Hoth was charged with responsibility for war crimes committed by his troops. Found guilty in 1948, he was sentenced to 15 years' imprisonment, but in the event served just six years.

Aged 69 on his release from Landsberg prison, Hermann Hoth spent his retirement writing on military history; he died at Goslar in 1971.

Major Erich Bärenfänger

A comparison between the career and fate of GenObst Hoth, who commanded the greatest armoured force ever led by a German general in Russia, and of this battalion commander also decorated with the Swords, is striking.

Born on 12 January 1915 at Menden, Westphalia, Erich Bärenfänger was conscripted into the new Wehrmacht as an enlisted man in 1936. After three years' service with Inf Regt 123 he was commissioned as Leutnant der Reserve in 1939. Just before he was due to be discharged on completion of his military service, war broke out. His unit saw action as part of 50.Inf Div in the Polish campaign. He distinguished himself as an infantry platoon leader in the West in spring 1940, suffering the first of many wounds and earning both classes of the Iron Cross. Rejoining his unit after a month in hospital, Bärenfänger saw fierce fighting in the Balkan campaign, in the breaking of the Metaxas Line and the advance through the Klidi and Klissura passes, before his unit moved to Romania in preparation for the invasion of the Soviet Union, for which it was assigned to Army Group South.

Not long after the Russian campaign opened Oberleutnant Bärenfänger was wounded in action once again, by an exploding land mine. Returning in September 1941 after hospital treatment, he was given command of 7 Kompanie/Inf Reg 123, which he led in the capture of enemy positions at Otshakov. Bärenfänger's courage and leadership were already making a strong impression on his superiors; and despite his modest rank, he was given command of his division's motorised spearhead unit.

Fighting alongside Romanian and Bulgarian troops as part of 11.Armee under GFM von Manstein, 50.Inf Div saw fierce combat on

A typical view of Hoth in the field with one of his staff officers during operations on the Eastern Front. Hoth habitually wore only his Knight's Cross, not attaching his many other decorations to his field uniform. After the so-called 'Death Ride of the 4th Panzer Army' at Kursk, Hoth remarked to Manstein: 'The Russians have learnt a lot since 1941. They are no longer peasants with simple minds. They have learnt the art of war from us.'

the Dnieper, at Kiev, and at Perekop and Sevastopol in the Crimea. On one occasion Bärenfänger led his men in driving an entire Soviet artillery regiment from its hilltop positions. During a single engagement near Sevastopol he was wounded three times, in the knee, legs and eyes; and in January 1942 he was awarded the Wound Badge in Gold. For his part in numerous actions Bärenfänger received the German Cross in Gold; and in June 1942, his name was added to the Roll of Honour of the German Army after he and his men had forced their way through minefields and bunker systems, in terrain broken by deep gullies, to seize a bridgehead at Kamyshli. On 7 August 1942, Bärenfänger was awarded the Knight's Cross; he was also decorated by his allies, with the Royal Bulgarian Gallantry Order and the Romanian Order of the Crown 5th Class with Swords. A few weeks after the award of his Knight's Cross he received a richly deserved promotion to Hauptmann, and was given command of III Bataillon of his regiment. He refused the home leave that was offered, preferring to stay with his men at a time of heavy fighting.

Subsequently, 50.Inf Div fought in the Caucasus and was nearly cut off in the Kuban bridgehead before escaping across the frozen Sea of Asov in February 1943. After retreating to the lower Dnieper the division returned to the Crimea, where on one occasion Hptm Bärenfänger even found himself for a short period city commandant of the port of Yalta. As the war turned against the Wehrmacht in Russia, Bärenfänger showed himself equally adept at defensive fighting as in the assault. During the spring of 1943 the collapse of Romanian units on his flank left his battalion exposed; he immediately led a counter-attack which routed two entire Soviet regiments, capturing many prisoners and much equipment. For this achievement he was awarded the Oak-Leaves on 17 May 1943, and promoted to Major.

The Germans clung on in the Crimea for the remainder of the year, and Bärenfänger received further multiple wounds during furious defensive actions and counter-attacks through the autumn and winter. Once again he refused evacuation for treatment, and insisted on remaining with his unit. In early January 1944 his divisional commander, GenMaj Sixt, recommended Maj Bärenfänger for the Swords. The award of this decoration on 23 January made him one of the youngest, most junior Army officers to receive it; he was promoted to Oberstleutnant a week later, and named regimental commander – an appointment that was highly popular with his men. Bärenfänger was shortly afterwards recalled to Germany for a regimental commanders' training course, and on its completion – unfortunately for his men, but fortunately for him –

Major Erich Bärenfänger in the official portrait taken after the award of the Oak-Leaves in May 1943, when he was commander of III/Gren Regt 123 fighting with 50.Inf Div in the Crimea.

it was decided that in view of his distinguished service and many wounds he was not to return to the front. Instead he was posted as inspector of the Hitler Youth Military Preparatory Camps, where the older boys of the HJ were trained for military service. In his absence, 50.Inf Div was virtually wiped out.

In the final stages of the war the desperate shortage of experienced combat leaders took Bärenfänger back to the front line once again. He was given a combat role in the defence of Berlin, and in April 1945 he was promoted to Generalmajor – the youngest in the German Army, having just turned 30 years of age. When GenMaj Bärenfänger's last desperate attempt to lead a break-out from the capital failed, on 1 May, rather than allow themselves to be captured by the Soviets, Erich Bärenfänger and his wife committed suicide.

Oberstleutnant Dr Franz Bäke

Born on 28 February 1898 at Schwarzenfels, Franz Bäke volunteered for Inf Regt 53 in May 1915. He served throughout the rest of World War I, being wounded in action and earning the Iron Cross Second Class while still a teenager. After being wounded he was transferred to Art Regt 7, reaching the rank of Vizefeldwebel and potential officer candidate. Demobilized in January 1919, Bäke took up medical studies, specializing in dentistry and qualifying as a dentist in 1923; in the meantime he saw some action with Freikorps Epp. He opened his own dental practice, but was commissioned as a Leutnant der Reserve in December 1937. He served as a reservist with the reconnaissance battalion Aufklärungs Abteilung 6 until August 1939, when he was transferred to active service as a platoon commander with an anti-tank unit, Panzerjäger Abteilung 65. Bäke took part in the occupation of the Sudetenland as deputy

Maj Franz Bäke in the turret of his Befehlswagen IV command tank (whose markings are unknown, though by regulation it should have been numbered 'R01' or 'R00'). He displays the Oak-Leaves awarded on 1 August 1943 as regimental commander of Pz Regt 11. Of special interest are the three badges for single-handed destruction of an enemy tank worn on his right sleeve. On 11 July, during the Kursk offensive, 6.Pz Div was serving with Army Detachment Kempf as part of the northwards drive towards Prokhorovka. Bäke was leading a tank column (headed by a captured T-34, for deception) in an attempt to seize a vital bridge over the Donets river. Surrounded after dark by a number of Soviet tanks, Bäke left his command tank (which had no main gun) and led a successful attack on foot using Haft-Hl 3 'Panzerknacker' magnetic anti-tank charges, personally destroying three T-34s.

commander of 3 Kompanie. He saw service during the Polish campaign, and in November 1939, promoted to Oberleutnant der Reserve, he took over his unit's 1 Kompanie. In this capacity he saw considerable action with 6.Pz Div during the 1940 campaign, being wounded twice and earning the Iron Cross First Class.

In February 1941, Bäke was appointed to the regimental staff of his division's Pz Regt 11, and in May was promoted to Hauptmann. He saw continuous action on the northern sector during the first phase of the invasion of Russia, when his regiment reached the outskirts of Leningrad by 9 September before being shifted south to the Moscow front. In December 1941, Bäke was given command of his regiment's I Btl, moving to II/Pz Regt 11 in April 1942 when this battalion was withdrawn to France for re-equipment. Promoted Major that August, Bäke was back in Russia in November 1942, and shortly afterwards saw hard fighting with 4.Panzerarmee during the attempt to relieve Stalingrad. On 11 January 1943 he was awarded the Knight's Cross for distinguished leadership.

The well-known but interesting formal portrait of Obst Bäke after the award of the Swords; at the time he was a regimental commander, but he would soon command a Panzer brigade which would see action on both Western and Eastern Fronts, and in the last weeks of the war he would be promoted Generalmajor and given the remnants of a division. This is one of only a handful of known photos which show the extremely rare Panzer Battle Badge for 100 engagements with the enemy being worn. Together with his Knight's Cross with Oak-Leaves and Swords, his Wound Badge in Gold, and his three sleeve badges for single-handed destruction of a tank with hand-held weapons, this almost certainly made Franz Bäke's uniform unique in the Wehrmacht.

For the Kursk offensive of July 1943, 6.Pz Div was one of three armoured divisions serving with Army Detachment Kempf on the right of 4.Panzerarmee in Manstein's Army Group South. On the night of 11/12 July, Franz Bäke seized a vital bridge over the Donets at Rzhavets by a daring *coup de main*, displaying in the process extraordinary personal courage (see caption to accompanying photograph). On the 13th he was wounded, but stayed with his unit. On the 14th, Maj Bäke was given temporary command of Pz Regt 11, although technically too junior; there was tacit acknowledgement that if he continued to perform well, confirmation and promotion would follow. His performance lived up to all hopes, and on 1 August 1943 Maj Bäke was awarded the Oak-Leaves. He retained his temporary post until 1 November 1943, when he was confirmed in his command and promoted Oberstleutnant.

Bäke would remain as regimental commander until July 1944, and during the winter fighting of 1943/44 he would yet again distinguish himself. He was given command of a battle group, named for him as Panzer Regiment Bäke, which comprised surviving Tiger tanks from sPzAbt 503, his battalion of Panthers from Pz Regt 11, self-propelled assault guns and armoured engineer units. In a sustained five-day battle around Balabonovka in January 1944, this unit destroyed 267 Soviet armoured vehicles while losing just one Tiger and four of its Panthers. Bäke was personally awarded the Swords by Hitler on 21 February 1944. On 26 April ObstLt Bäke also received the very rare class of the Panzer Battle Badge for 100 engagements with the enemy; he is reported to have received this, too, from Hitler's hands.

On 1 May 1944, Bäke was promoted to Oberst, and in July was appointed to command Panzerbrigade 106 'Feldherrnhalle', operating first on the Western Front and then transferring back to the East. (It was only on 1 January 1945 that his status was officially changed from a reserve to a regular officer.) His brigade took part in the ill-fated offensive around Lake Balaton, Hungary; and in late January he left the front for a divisional commander's training course which lasted until early March. On 9 March he was appointed temporary commander of 13.Pz Div, still in the rank of Oberst; but his regular commission as a career soldier (Berufsoldat) now allowed promotion to Generalmajor, which followed on 20 April, with confirmation of his divisional command.[2]

General Bäke went into captivity at the end of the war while fighting on the Austrian front. After his eventual release in 1950 he returned to his pre-war profession, opening up a dentistry practice. He was killed in an automobile accident at Hagen on 12 December 1978.

Hauptmann Gerhard Barkhorn

'Gerd' Barkhorn was born in Königsberg, East Prussia, on 20 May 1919. He joined the Luftwaffe in 1937 as an 18-year-old officer candidate. After completing his flying training he was posted to JG 2 'Richthofen'. On 1 August 1940, Leutnant Barkhorn was posted to 6/JG 52 flying Bf 109s on the Western Front following the fall of France. His introduction to combat flying was far from auspicious; he failed to gain any aerial victories during the Battle of Britain, and had to be rescued after being shot down and forced to ditch in the Channel.

It was only while flying his 120th combat sortie, during the invasion of the USSR, that he gained his first "kill", a DB-3, on 2 July 1941. It was three weeks later before he scored again, shooting down an I-16 on 28 July. By 22

Germany's – and history's – second greatest fighter ace, surpassed only by Erich Hartmann, and one of only two pilots ever to achieve 300 kills, Hauptmann Gerhard Barkhorn is seen here as Staffelkapitän of 4/JG 52 after the award of the Oak-Leaves for his 100th aerial victory. It is worth noting that neither he nor Hartmann went on to senior rank or command, remaining on the Russian Front and devoting themselves to combat.

---

[2] This involved command of a largely theoretical formation, Pz Div 'Feldherrnhalle 2', constructed on paper from the remnants of 13.Pz Div and 60.PzGren Div 'Feldherrnhalle'.

One of several Bf 109G-6 fighters flown by Barkhorn as commander of II/JG 52 in 1943–44. His characteristic markings were his wife's name 'Christl', and a small number '5' associated with the Gruppenkommandeur's double chevron tactical marking.

August he had finally reached five confirmed kills; from then on his score would rise gradually rather than dramatically, as he gained experience and confidence over the coming months. By January 1942 he had achieved 30 victories, and on 1 March was appointed as Staffelkapitän of 4/JG 52; Barkhorn had gradually proved himself to be a rock-solid member of his unit. On 25 July 1942 he was wounded during a dog-fight; but by August his tally had reached 64, for which he was awarded the Knight's Cross on 23 August. Barkhorn did score occasional multiple victories – four during one mission, and his personal best of seven in one day – but most of his successes came in small numbers and with great regularity.

Following the award of the Knight's Cross he was given a break from combat flying for about two months, returning to the front in October 1942. During that month he added a further 14 victories to his tally, mostly Yak 1 or LaGG 3 fighters. Seven more victories were scored in November, and on 19 December an American Lend-Lease P-40 became his 100th victim. The Oak-Leaves were awarded on 11 January 1943, by which date Barkhorn had increased his score to 105 victories. It continued to mount steadily: 15 in February, 6 in March, 7 in May, 4 in June, 1 in July – and then a phenomenally successful August 1943, during which he downed 24 enemy aircraft including his 150th kill, an Il-2 Sturmovik on 8 August.

Now holding the rank of Hauptmann, Barkhorn was appointed Gruppenkommandeur of II/JG 52 in September 1943, and added another 15 victories to his log-book during that month. On 30 November a Yak-1 fighter became his 200th victim; and on 23 January 1944, Hptm Barkhorn became the first German fighter pilot to have flown

2,000 combat sorties. Despite the increasing quality of both aircraft and pilots available to the Red Air Force as the war continued, Barkhorn seemed to respond by shooting down even more of them. After only another ten weeks he raised his score from 200 to 250, with another Yak 1 on 13 February 1944 – he was only the second pilot in history to achieve this number of victories, which brought the award of the Swords on 2 March 1944.

The strain of almost continual combat flying took its toll, however, and Barkhorn's Bf 109G-6 was 'bounced' and shot down by Soviet fighters on 31 May 1944, during his sixth sortie of the day. Badly wounded, he was taken off flying duties for several months. Returning to combat flying in October 1944, by the 14th of that month he had raised his score to 275.

In mid January 1945, with an astonishing total of 301 victories to his name, Hptm Barkhorn was posted to the Fw 190-equipped JG 6 in Germany, which had suffered serious losses among its leaders on 1 January during the ill-conceived 'Bodenplatte' ground attack operation

This photo of Boerst in the operations room of his Gruppe shows him wearing the *Frontflugspange für Kampfflieger* over the left breast pocket. The pendant below the winged bomb central motif indicates that he had flown over 500 combat missions at this time.

against Allied airfields. However, Barkhorn was found to be still suffering too badly from the effects of his wounds, and was taken off flying duties again and sent to hospital. On his release, in mid April Barkhorn made his way to München-Riem airfield and joined the famous Jagdverband 44, the so-called 'Aces Squadron' flying Me 262 jet fighters under the leadership of GenLt Adolf Galland. On 21 April, Barkhorn was involved in an attack on enemy bombers when one of his engines failed. As he turned and headed for home, his speed much reduced, he was attacked by two enemy fighters and forced down. He survived a crash-landing in a field, but his injuries kept him in hospital during the closing days of the war. His tally of 301 kills made him the second most successful fighter pilot of all time, second only to his JG 52 comrade Erich Hartmann.

Barkhorn joined the reborn German Air Force after the war, and retrained for jet flying with his former enemies, the Royal Air Force. He reached the rank of Generalleutnant before finally retiring in 1976. General Barkhorn and his wife died tragically in an automobile accident in January 1983.

Major Alwin Boerst

Alwin Boerst began his military service in April 1934 when he joined a transport unit; he left the Army as an Unteroffizier in October 1935, but in 1937 he volunteered for the Luftwaffe and joined with his previous rank. After serving with Kampfgeschwader 157 he was soon selected for officer training. With the rank of Oberfähnrich, he joined 3 Staffel of Stukageschwader 163, and while serving with this dive-bomber unit was commissioned Leutnant on 1 September 1938.

Boerst completed no fewer than 39 combat sorties during the brief Polish campaign. In action again during the offensive in the West, Boerst racked up 113 combat missions, and in August 1940 was promoted to Oberleutnant. He went on to fly in combat over the Balkans and Crete in spring/summer 1941 – a notably successful campaign for the Stukas. Unlike fighter pilots, who were rewarded for the number of enemy aircraft they had shot down, bomber pilots had no such obvious method of making a mark. The Junkers Ju 87 Stuka, though first class in its designed role as a dive-bomber, was easy meat for Allied fighters, being slow and lightly armed, and needed its own fighter protection. Losses in combat were heavy, and bomber pilots were usually decorated based on the number of combat sorties they had successfully completed. During the attack on Crete, however, Boerst was able to achieve an easily verifiable success when he sank one Royal Navy destroyer and badly damaged another.

By the time Germany invaded the Soviet Union in June 1941, OLt Boerst was Staffelkapitän of 3/StG 2 'Immelmann'. Here again Boerst scored some verifiable successes, including the destruction of a vital bridge over the Dnieper. In the first few weeks he destroyed around 80 enemy vehicles, six tanks, a train and several gun emplacements. On 5 October 1941, after completing 300 sorties, Boerst was decorated with the Knight's Cross.

Shortly after completing his 600th combat mission in September 1942. Boerst was rotated back to a home posting as an instructor. On 28 November 1942 Boerst added the Oak-Leaves to his Knight's Cross, and three days later he was promoted to Hauptmann. A well-earned period of home leave followed; but early in 1943 he returned to the front line, joining 3/SG 3 (some Stuka units were now being redesignated Schlachtgeschwader, 'battle wings'). His Gruppe had recently been almost annihilated in Tunisia, and had been withdrawn for re-equipment before deploying to the East. In early October 1943, Boerst was severely wounded in the leg by anti-aircraft fire; and on returning to duty he took over as Gruppenkommandeur of I/StG 2 'Immelmann'. By this date many Stukagruppen were being re-equipped with fighter-bomber versions of the single-seat Fw 190, but I/StG 2 was still flying Ju 87Ds. On 29 January 1944, Alwin Boerst flew his 1,000th combat sortie.

On 30 March 1944, Hptm Boerst took off for his first mission flying the new Ju 87G-1, a Stuka modified as a 'tank-buster' with big 40mm cannon mounted under each wing. During an attack on Soviet tanks north of Jassy, Boerst's *Kanonenvogel* was shot down and he and his gunner were killed. On 6 April 1944, Hptm Boerst was posthumously awarded the Swords.

Hauptmann Alwin Boerst in a formal portrait following the award of the Oak-Leaves in November 1942. Boerst was one of a select band of airmen decorated with the Oak-Leaves for their achievements while flying the effective but obsolete Junkers Ju 87 Stuka.

SS-Brigadeführer u.Generalmajor der Waffen-SS Hermann Priess

Hermann Priess was born on 24 May 1901 at Marnitz in Mecklenburg, the son of a farmer. On completion of his schooling he worked on the family farm until January 1919, when he enlisted in the Army as a volunteer – the war on the Western Front was over, but Germany was torn by armed unrest and her eastern and northern frontiers were threatened. He served in Freikorps von Brandis in the Baltic theatre, and was wounded during the fighting for Riga, winning both classes of the Iron Cross.[3]

SS-Oberführer Hermann Priess, seen here after the award of his Knight's Cross in April 1943 as commander of SS-Pz Artillerie Regt 3 in the SS 'Totenkopf' Division. Interestingly he still wears the old style collar patches for this rank, which officially went out of use in 1942.

Priess joined the SS-Verfügungstruppe – the first military units of the SS – in 1934, and served as the company commander of 13 (Infanterie-geschütz) Kompanie/ SS-Regt 'Germania'. When the decision was taken to add an artillery regiment to the SS-VT, Priess was heavily involved in the establishment and training of this new unit. He and his gunners saw service in the Polish campaign in support of the Army's Panzer-verband Ostpreussen, and Priess received the 1939 Iron Cross. Subsequently he was transferred to the newly formed 'Totenkopf' Division, formed from SS-Totenkopfverbände security troops, and, with the rank of SS-Sturmbannführer (Major), took command of II Abteilung of the division's artillery regiment. Shortly after the conclusion of the campaign in the West, Priess was promoted to command the regiment.

Priess distinguished himself in combat on the Eastern Front when the 'Totenkopf' Division was encircled in the Demjansk Pocket in winter 1941/42. The divisional commander, SS-Ogruf Theodor Eicke, was particularly impressed by the achievements of Priess's gunners during these furious defensive actions, and remarked, 'If it wasn't for Priess, none of us would still be here'. When Eicke was killed on 26 February 1943, Priess was given command of the division with the rank of SS-Oberführer (Brigadier). For his division's service in bitter fighting against the Soviet 3rd Tank Army, Priess received the Knight's Cross on 28 April 1943.

In the months that followed the 'Totenkopf' saw intensive combat, first in the third battle of Kharkov and then, in July, in the southern sector of the Kursk salient, where the division's Panzer regiment was heavily committed to the huge tank battles around Prokhorovka. The failure of the Kursk offensive was accompanied by a new Soviet attack on the Mius river, and by August the division was back around Kharkov, which would fall to the Red Army for the last time on the 22nd. On 9 September 1943, Priess was decorated with the Oak-Leaves. There was to be no respite for the 'Totenkopf', one of the handful of formations which Hitler now trusted. It remained on the Eastern Front for the rest

[3] See Elite 76, *The German Freikorps 1918–23*

of the war, seeing heavy combat in every crisis of that theatre and earning ungrudging praise from senior Wehrmacht commanders for its prowess in battle. On 24 April 1944, Hermann Priess was awarded the Swords. On 13 July he handed over command of his division to SS-Oberf Hellmuth Becker, and took over as commander of the newly formed XIII SS-Armeekorps. In fact, during its active service on the Western Front the corps contained only one SS formation, 17.SS-PzGren Div 'Götz von Berlichingen', alongside 11.Pz Div, parts of 3. & 15.PzGren Divs, and a number of Army Volksgrenadier divisions. These units were already war-weary and short of equipment, supplies and experienced men. Priess's corps went into action in September 1944 in an attempt to prevent the break-through by the US 3rd Army in the Saarland. In October, Priess handed over command SS-Gruf Max Simon, and took over I SS-Panzerkorps as it prepared for action in the forthcoming Ardennes offensive. Priess commanded the corps through the ill-fated Battle of the Bulge, and also during the final great offensive in Hungary, when the Germans launched their failed attempt to halt the Red Army around Lake Balaton in February–March 1945.

Priess survived the war, but was arraigned on war crimes charges, among them that troops under his command were responsible for the Malmedy massacre of US prisoners in the Ardennes. He was convicted in 1946 and sentenced to 20 years' imprisonment, but was released in 1954. He died at Ahrensburg on 2 March 1985.

SS-Gruppenführer Priess after the award of the Swords as commander of 3.SS-Pz Div 'Totenkopf' in April 1944. From its earliest campaign the 'Totenkopf' acquired a reputation for war crimes, but there is no denying that throughout its service in the East it was one of the most effective combat divisions in Russia.

Generalleutnant Smilo Freiherr von Lüttwitz

There could hardly be a more striking contrast than that between Priess and Baron von Lüttwitz, a professional soldier who has been held up as the epitome of the positive aspects of the German military character. During his career Lüttwitz served in the army of the Kaiser, in the Wehrmacht and in the Bundeswehr of the German Federal Republic.

Born on 23 December 1895 in Strasbourg, into a family with a long history of military service, he began his military life on 3 August 1914 when he became an officer cadet with Leib-Dragonerregiment Nr 24 (2.Grossherzoglich hessisches) at Darmstadt. The young cavalry cadet saw action on the Eastern Front during World War I, being wounded several times, and on 16 June 1915 he was granted his commission as Leutnant. In 1916, following the death in action of his brother, Lüttwitz served for two years as a staff officer at corps level and with Heeresgruppe Kronprinz. He returned to the front line in 1918 as an adjutant with the Darmstädter Dragoons, ending the war with both classes of the Iron Cross and the Wound Badge in Silver among other awards. After the Armistice he remained in the Reichsheer of the Weimar Republic, and was promoted Oberleutnant in 1925 while serving with 6.(Preussichen)

The road to Prokhorovka: a column of PzKw III Ausf L tanks from the 'Totenkopf' Division's SS-Pz Regt 3 move up for the Kursk offensive of July 1943. (Private collection)

Reiter Regiment. In 1930 he was promoted Rittmeister (Captain), and appointed as an Adjutant to the Kommando der Kraftfahrkampftruppen – the forerunner of the Panzerwaffe. In 1935, Major von Lüttwitz was given command of PzAufkl Abt 5; and in 1938–40 he filled staff posts with Heeresgruupe 4 in Leipzig and XV Armeekorps in Jena. In October 1939 he was promoted to Oberstleutnant, and saw staff service during the Polish campaign.

Shortly before the campaign in the West, Obstlt von Lüttwitz was given command of Schützen (later, PzGren) Regt 12, part of 4.Panzer Division. This formation spearheaded the invasion of Holland in May 1940; it saw particularly heavy fighting against British units around Lille, and later against the French in the Somme, Aisne and Loire sectors. After the French Armistice, Lüttwitz was promoted full colonel. For the invasion of Russia, Obst von Lüttwitz's division formed part of Panzergruppe 2 under GenObst Guderian in Army Group Centre; it fought in the crossings of the Beresina, Dnieper and Desna rivers, and finally in the costly attempt to capture Tula south of Moscow. The onset of the bitter winter of 1941/42 found them digging in to the east of Orel. For his skilled leadership during the advance, and for his personal gallantry during the defensive fighting at the end of the year, Obst von Lüttwitz was awarded the Knight's Cross on 14 January 1942. His divisional commander described him as 'the model of a regimental commander, always to be found where things are at their toughest'.

(Continued on page 41)

1

2

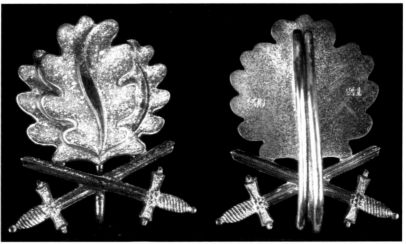

3

IM NAMEN
DES DEUTSCHEN VOLKES
VERLEIHE ICH
DEM GENERAL DER PANZERTRUPPE
ERWIN ROMMEL
DAS EICHENLAUB MIT SCHWERTERN
ZUM RITTERKREUZ
DES EISERNEN KREUZES

FÜHRERHAUPTQUARTIER
DEN 20. JANUAR 1942

DER FÜHRER
UND OBERSTE BEFEHLSHABER
DER WEHRMACHT

A

'PAPA' HOTH AT KURSK, JULY 1943

HERMANN FEGELEIN HUNTING PARTISANS, JUNE 1943

C

FRANZ BÄKE IN THE BALABANOVKA POCKET, JANUARY 1944

D

'GERD' BARKHORN'S 250TH VICTORY, 13 FEBRUARY 1944

'FIPS' PHILIPP OF THE 'GREEN HEARTS', MARCH 1942

F

ERICH RUDORFFER IN KARELIA, JUNE 1944

G

OTTO WEIDINGER AT THE FLORISDORFER BRIDGE, 9 APRIL 1945

On 1 April 1942, Lüttwitz was posted to 23.Inf Div, then stationed in Belgium, with the task of completely rebuilding it as the new 26.Panzer Division. On 1 September 1942 he was promoted to Generalmajor commanding; but his new armoured division was not sent into the line for another year. Committed to the Italian front in 1943, it was soon in combat against US forces after the Salerno landings. Promoted to Generalleutnant on 1 October, Lüttwitz displayed his old flair for leading his troops from the front, often taking his Kubelwagen jeep – or even a solo motorcycle – right into the thick of the fighting to get accurate situation reports. (Apart from anything else, this was good for the morale of any troops who saw him.) When Allied units tried to roll over the Germans on the left flank of 26.Pz Div, GenLt von Lüttwitz personally led his armoured reconnaissance battalion into an immediate and successful counter-attack. For this action Lüttwitz was mentioned in Wehrmacht despatches, and on 16 March 1944 he was awarded the Oak-Leaves. By that date he had received a severe eye injury during an Allied bombing raid in February 1944.

After hospital treatment to save his sight, Lüttwitz returned to combat duties in July, taking command of XLVI Panzerkorps on the Eastern Front; he was awarded the Swords on the 4th of that month, and was simultaneously promoted General der Panzertruppe. His new corps was almost completely encircled near Lemberg in Galicia by the great Soviet summer offensive which smashed through Army Group Centre. Lüttwitz led his corps in a fighting retreat back to positions on the Vistula in the vicinity of Warsaw. In September 1944, Gen von Lüttwitz was appointed to command 9.Armee. In January 1945 he faced a massed attack out of the Baranov bridgehead by Soviet units which had attained an 11-to-1 superiority in men, 7-to-1 in tanks and 20-to-1 in artillery. Army Group Centre is estimated to have lost between 350,000 and 400,000 men in the onslaught which followed, as German units were simply swept aside or crushed. General von Lüttwitz had already made his opinion about this hopeless situation known, both to his own superiors in the chain of command and also to Hitler himself. Enraged at such 'defeatism', Hitler had Lüttwitz removed from his command and summoned before a court martial. While enquiries were made he was posted to command a second-line formation, LXXXV Armeekorps, where he sat out the remaining weeks of the war. During this period he had to endure not only the knowledge that such investigations could lead to a death sentence, but also the news of his son's death in action in the Courland Pocket.

After the war, Gen von Lüttwitz was persuaded to don uniform once again to help build the Bundeswehr. He served with the rank of

An extremely able soldier, Baron von Lüttwitz was one of the generals who incurred Hitler's wrath by speaking openly and critically about the deteriorating situation on the Eastern Front. He was removed from his command in January 1945, at a time when men of his ability were most needed.

Generalleutnant Smilo Freiherr von Lüttwitz as commander of XLVI PZ Korps on the Russian Front in summer 1944. The previous February he had very nearly lost his sight due to injuries sustained during an Allied bombing raid in Italy.

Generalleutnant, finally retiring in 1960. Amongst his many decorations were the US Legion of Merit, and the Grand Cross of the German Federal Merit Order with Breast Star. Smilo von Lüttwitz died in retirement in May 1975 at the age of 79, and was buried with full military honours.

SS-Gruppenführer u.Generalleutnant der Waffen-SS Hermann Fegelein

Born in Bavaria on 30 October 1906, Fegelein was raised in Munich where his father, a retired officer, worked at a military riding school. After leaving university he fulfilled brief military service in 1925–26 with Reiter Regt 17, then served in the police 1927–29. He kept up a keen interest in equestrian sports, competing at international level. When he joined the Allgemeine-SS in 1933 he was commissioned SS-Untersturmführer and assigned to the cavalry branch, and by July 1937, aged only 30, he was commander of the SS Main Riding School in the rank of SS-Standartenführer (Colonel). A favourite of Himmler, he was allowed to retain this rank semi-officially when he joined the Waffen-SS in 1939 as commander of the new SS-Totenkopf Reiterstandarte 1. Deployed in Poland on security duties, the unit committed its first confirmed atrocities in October 1939.

This single regiment was gradually increased to brigade status, and served in the rear areas on the central sector of the Eastern Front from the early stages of Operation 'Barbarossa'. During anti-partisan duties under Himmler's Kommandostab RFSS, Fegelein's SS-Kavallerie Brigade committed widespread war crimes in the region of the Pripet Marshes in summer 1941. Transferred to front line duty, the brigade faced serious opposition in winter 1941/42, and fought well under 9.Armee command in desperate battles around Rzhev. Reduced to a 700-man battle group by March 1942, it was then progressively withdrawn to Poland by August that year, and SS-Staf Fegelein was awarded the Knight's Cross on 2 March 1942. In May, Fegelein was given a staff posting as inspector of SS cavalry, but returned to the front in December 1942 to lead a Kampfgruppe on the Don Front as part of Army Group B. On 20 December, Fegelein led an assault with two self-propelled guns on a Soviet corps HQ, capturing senior officers and important documents. Over the following two days Fegelein suffered two bullet wounds, and on 22 December he was awarded the Oak-Leaves.

Fegelein was promoted to SS-Brigadeführer und Generalmajor der Waffen-SS on 1 May 1942, and two weeks later took command of the SS-Kavallerie Division (later numbered 8., and titled 'Florian Geyer'), which had been created by expanding his old brigade. Fegelein led the division with some success during 1943, on anti-partisan operations in central Russia and later in the front line under Army Group South. He seems to have made up for his lack of staff training by relying upon competent and experienced subordinates, acknowledging his debt and assisting their careers. His personal bravery under fire seems to be well documented, and he qualified for the Close Combat Clasp in Silver. He was wounded again in September; and in January 1944, with the rank of SS-Gruppenführer, he joined the Führerhauptquartier as Himmler's liaison officer with Hitler.

Hermann Fegelein as an SS-Oberführer, awarded the Oak-Leaves for his command of a battle group on the Eastern Front in December 1942. In operations against the Soviet partisans and Red Army stragglers who swarmed in the Pripet Marshes behind Army Group Centre's front lines, mounted cavalry units such as his brigade were still effective.

In June 1944 he married Gretl Braun, sister of Hitler's mistress Eva. He was wounded once again in the assassination attempt on Hitler on 20 July 1944, and on that very day was decorated by Hitler with the Swords in recognition of his command of the 'Florian Geyer' Division. Despite his connections, however, Fegelein did not survive the paranoia which reigned in the Führerbunker in the closing days of the war, when Hitler was enraged to learn that Himmler – his 'loyal Heinrich' – had been exploring the possibility of secret negotiations with the Allies in the hope of saving his own neck. On 27 April 1945, Fegelein went missing from his post; he was apparently discovered with a mistress in a nearby apartment, drunk, in civilian clothes, and in possession of a substantial amount of money and false passports. He was dragged back to the Bunker and interrogated by the chief of the Gestapo, Heinrich Müller. Hitler ordered an immediate court-martial; and on 29 April, stripped of his insignia and decorations, Hermann Fegelein was shot by a firing squad of SS guards in the garden of the Foreign Office.

Major Erich Rudorffer

Rudorffer, born in Zwickau on 1 November 1917, joined the Luftwaffe in January 1940 at the age of 23. After completing his training he was posted to I Gruppe/JG 2 'Richthofen' as an NCO pilot. Within just four months of joining his unit Rudorffer was flying Bf 109s in action on the Western Front, and on 14 May he shot down his first enemy aircraft, a French Curtiss Hawk 75 fighter. On 26 May he shot down his first Spitfire, and went on to achieve a total of nine 'kills' before the surrender of France.

Over the next year Rudorffer's score grew slowly but steadily, through the Battle of Britain and the months that followed; by May 1941, it stood at 19 victories. Now commissioned as a Leutnant, he was awarded the Knight's Cross on 1 May 1941. Alongside JG 26, JG 2 remained on the Channel coast after the invasion of Russia took most of the Jagdwaffe eastwards. Rudorffer continued to record successes during the intermittent battles with RAF Fighter Command over the Channel and northern France, and his tally reached 40 on 8 December 1941. Rudorffer often displayed considerable chivalry in combat; on one occasion he actually escorted a heavily damaged RAF Hurricane back over the Channel after a dog-fight, ready to radio a report if the pilot came down in the sea – a compliment which was returned only days later, when he himself was shot up and escorted home by an RAF fighter.

In April 1942, II/JG 2 converted from the Messerschmitt Bf 109 to the superior new radial-engined Focke-Wulf Fw 190. At the head of 6 Staffel, Rudorffer took to his new mount with ease, and continued to fly regular missions against the RAF and – towards the end of the year –

A formal portrait of SS-Brigadeführer Fegelein as commander of 8.SS-Kav Div 'Florian Geyer'. Over his breast pocket he wears the Close Combat Clasp in Silver, awarded for a cumulative total of at least 30 days' close quarter fighting. Although Fegelein probably owed his Oak-Leaves and Swords more to his connections than to genuine military ability, he was not without personal courage, and was wounded in action several times.

against the first USAAF bomber raids over France. He was recovering from a wound when, in December 1942, his Gruppe was transferred to Tunisia following the Allied landings in French North Africa. He rejoined his unit at Bizerta on 17 December, shooting down two fighters the next day. He took over as Gruppenkommandeur on 8 January 1943, and demonstrated cool leadership as well as extraordinary personal flying and marksmanship. Always taking off last, so as to have the best information before engaging, he specialized in diving past the enemy and then zooming up under them, closing to as little as 50 yards before firing. In one action on 9 February he shot down eight USAAF fighters, six of them in the space of just seven minutes; and on 15 February he downed a further seven Allied aircraft in just 20 minutes. A Flying Fortress on 12 March was the last of his 26 kills in Tunisia. Returning to France a few days later, Hauptmann Rudorffer was confirmed in command of II/JG 2, which now reconverted from the Fw 190A to the Bf 109G-6. (The arrival on the scene of increasingly heavy US daylight bomber formations with shorter-ranged escorts demanded new tactics by a mixed force of the two fighter types.)

Erich Rudorffer, seen here after the award of the Knight's Cross in May 1941 for having scored 19 victories over French and British aircraft in the *Westfeldzug* and the Battle of Britain while flying Bf 109Es with JG 2 'Richthofen' (whose cuff title he wears on his right sleeve). During his combat career – which after April 1942 was spent mostly flying Fw 190As with JG 54 – Rudorffer flew over 1,000 missions. When this portrait was taken there was nothing to mark him out from many other moderately successful fighter pilots, but by the end of the war in Europe his skills would be legendary. In February–May 1945 he led the Me 262A jet fighter Gruppe I/JG 7 on home defence duties, and achieved no fewer than 12 personal jet kills in the last weeks of the war. This made him Germany's third-equal daytime jet ace (with Ofw Hermann Buchner and Maj Georg-Peter Eder).

An exhausted-looking Major Rudorffer wearing the Swords awarded in January 1945 after his score reached 210 kills, many of them multiple victories achieved on single days over the Eastern Front – his record was 13 in one day. It has often been claimed that the phenomenal scores achieved by German aces were due solely to their facing obsolete aircraft flown by ill-trained pilots during the opening phases of the invasion of the USSR in 1941. However, Erich Rudorffer did not reach the Eastern Front until 1943, when the technical and human opposition was of a far higher standard. His final tally of 222 included 58 of the notorious Il-2 Stormovik armoured ground-attack aircraft; and in the West and the Mediterranean, 40 Spitfires, 7 P-38s and 10 B-17 Flying Fortresses.

—

In summer 1943, Rudorffer was tasked with the formation of a new IV Gruppe of the famous JG 54 'Grünherz'. In fact, he was posted to Russia after a few weeks to take command of II/JG 54 after that Gruppe's commander was killed, and he would therefore continue to fly the Fw 190. It was on the Eastern Front that Rudorffer would come to prominence as not simply one of many successful fighter pilots, but one of Germany's leading aces.

Not long after his arrival, on 24 August 1943, he succeeded in shooting down five Soviet aircraft on his first sortie of the day. After refuelling and re-arming he took off again, and added three more kills during his second sortie. Rudorffer's ability to score multiple victories would soon be the stuff of legend. On 14 September he shot down five aircraft; and on 11 October, seven within just seven minutes, taking his total over 100. On 6 November 1943, in an astonishing display of virtuosity, he downed 13 Soviet aircraft in just 17 minutes, securing his place as one of the great fighter 'Experten'.

Rudorffer continued to achieve the occasional spectacular success while pushing up his overall score. On 7 April 1944, six aircraft fell to his guns during a single sortie. Finally, with his 134th kill, Hptm Rudorffer was decorated with the Oak-Leaves. This brought a welcome trip back to Germany for the official investiture, but he was soon back in the front line. On 3 July 1944 he downed five aircraft, and on the 26th, six more. On 28 October, Rudorffer was returning from a combat mission and about to land when he spotted an approaching formation of Soviet Il-2 Stormovik ground-attack aircraft – heavily armoured, armed with cannon, and notoriously difficult to shoot down. Aborting his landing, within just ten minutes he had shot down nine Il-2s and driven the rest away. On a second mission he added a further two kills, to bring his score to 11 for the day. On 26 January 1945, after scoring his 210th aerial victory, Erich Rudorffer received the Oak-Leaves with Swords to his Knight's Cross.

His expertise earned Major Rudorffer a transfer back to Germany to command I/JG 7, equipped with the revolutionary Me 262 jet fighter. Pilot training on this lightning-fast but immature aircraft was difficult and dangerous, but Rudorffer soon mastered it. During the last weeks of the Third Reich he became one of the world's first jet aces, credited with 12 kills while flying the Me 262. His last victory, over a B-17 heavy bomber, brought his overall total to 222 enemy aircraft destroyed in air combat, making him the seventh highest scoring fighter ace of all time. He was shot down himself 16 times, crash-landing successfully on seven of these occasions and baling out nine times. He is reported never to have taken leave during his service on the Eastern Front, apart from required attendance at the investiture ceremonies for his awards.

Rudorffer's phenomenal flying career was still not over. He joined the post-war German Air Force, and subsequently became an airline pilot before finally retiring.

Generalmajor Max Sachsenheimer

Born on 5 December 1909 at Mühlbach in Baden, Sachsenheimer volunteered for military service in 1927 after completing his schooling. Serving with Inf Regt 14, he was promoted to NCO status as a potential officer candidate, and after undergoing officer training he was commissioned Leutnant in 1934. He was posted to Inf Regt 75, a unit of 5.Inf Div; and two years later, as an Oberleutnant, he took part in the re-occupation of the Rhineland.

Sachsenheimer saw his first combat during the campaign in the West where, leading a forward assault group, he was responsible for successfully capturing several bridges over the Seine, earning himself both classes of the Iron Cross. In January 1941 he was promoted to Hauptmann, and sent on a staff course. Shortly after the invasion of the Soviet Union, on 26 July 1941, Sachsenheimer once again took up a combat command, leading II Btl of his old regiment. He saw much intensive action in the Vyazma area, and during one attack by Soviet infantry and armour his left hand was almost torn off by shell fragments. He was evacuated for specialist treatment in Berlin; and he had hardly returned to the Eastern Front when, in December 1941, 5.Inf Div was withdrawn to France for re-organization as a Jäger (light infantry) division.

In January 1942 the new 5.Jäger Division drew winter clothing and returned to Russia, where it went into action around Staraya Russa in the Leningrad sector. Apart from the freezing conditions and the

A group of Army officers are congratulated by Hitler on the award of the Oak-Leaves; at far left is Max Sachsenheimer, commander of Jäger Regt 75 – note the traditional Jäger oak sprig insignia worn on his right sleeve.

Soviet counter-offensive, the biggest problem the division faced was an epidemic of typhus spread by the lice with which most of the troops soon became infested in the foul conditions. Both the division's senior medical officers fell victim to the disease while treating their comrades. In March 1942, Sachsenheimer's battalion played a significant part in the fighting to break the encirclement at Demjansk, and his leadership was rewarded with the Knight's Cross on 11 April. His typically modest response was that 'There can be no performance by an officer that is not made possible by his soldiers'.

In the summer of 1942 Sachsenheimer was given temporary command of Jäger Regt 75 in the absence of its commander. A short spell of leave followed; when he returned, his battalion was temporarily under the command of GenMaj Eugen Meindl's Parachute Division, engaged in security operations against the swarms of Soviet partisans and Red Army stragglers. In October 1942, Sachsenheimer contracted a serious illness which resulted in his being evacuated once again; he remained at the military hospital in Freiburg until February 1943. During his time in hospital he was promoted to Major, and shortly afterwards received the German Cross in Gold.

Not long after his return to 5.Jäger Div its new commander, GenMaj Thumm, recommended Sachsenheimer for General Staff training. This commenced in October 1943 at Hirschberg, and on its completion he returned to his division to take command of Jäger Regiment 75. At the head of his regiment Sachsenheimer then saw fierce fighting around Orscha and Brest Litovsk. On 1 April 1944 he was promoted to Oberstleutnant, and on 14 May was awarded the Oak-Leaves for his distinguished leadership at both battalion and regimental level. In August 1944 he was selected for a divisional commander's course, again at Hirschberg. On its completion Sachsenheimer was promoted to Oberst, and on 10 September 1944 he given command of 17. Inf Div, which had been pushed back into southern Poland by the great Soviet summer offensive. This Bavarian division was a good formation, but it had taken severe casualties both in winter 1941/42 with Army Group Centre and in the southern Ukraine in 1943. His initial performance as divisional commander brought Obst Saschsenheimer promotion to Generalmajor on 1 December 1944.

Barely six weeks later, a massive new Soviet offensive virtually annihilated the division, reducing it to barely 1,000 soldiers. Among them was GenMaj Sachsenheimer, who earned the respect of his men by always being found in the thick of the fighting. The fit survivors of the division were so few that its remnant was actually subordinated to a pioneer battalion. They were committed to the defence of Breslau in Czechoslovakia – the object of one of Hitler's

The burly-looking Max Sachsenheimer was a popular and respected battalion and regimental commander who gave the credit for his awards to the men he led, insisting that any successes achieved by an officer were made possible only by the efforts of his soldiers. Shortly after the award of the Oak-Leaves he was selected for divisional command.

insane orders for resistance 'to the last man and the last bullet'. On 6 February 1945, Sachsenheimer was decorated with the Swords for his personal gallantry and distinguished leadership. Six days later he was finally given freedom of action, and determined to lead as many of his men as possible out of the doomed city. A Kampfgruppe of around 1,400 men made the break-out attempt; about 800 of these reached German lines under Sachsenheimer's leadership.

Sachsenheimer was subsequently given command of a newly 'rebuilt' 17.Inf Div, and with this largely theoretical formation he was tasked with defending the Görlitzer Heide in the closing days of the war. After the surrender Sachsenheimer and some of his officers and men made their way through Soviet-held territory and successfully reached US lines. Unlike many soldiers whose term in captivity was very brief, as a general officer and divisional commander Sachsenheimer was held for just under two years. After his release he worked initially as a gardener, then as a salesman for construction materials, before going into business for himself. Max Sachsenheimer died on 2 June 1973 at Merzhausen near Freiburg.

Oberstleutnant Heinz-Georg Lemm

Born in Schwerin in June 1919, Lemm became an officer cadet in 1935 and attended the Kriegsschule in Munich. Commissioned as a Leutnant, he joined Inf Regt 27, part of the Mecklenberg 12.Infanterie Division. He fought in the Polish campaign, during which the Colonel-in-Chief of the division's artillery regiment, the anti-Nazi former Army Commander GenObst Werner von Fritsch, joined the division and deliberately got himself killed in action. During the attack on France and the Low Countries in May 1940, 12.Inf Div served under 4.Armee advancing through Luxembourg, to the Somme, Nantes and the Vendée. Lemm was involved in fierce hand-to-hand fighting when the division resisted Allied attempts to cut the rear lines of the advancing Panzer units, and after one engagement a bayonet wound put him in a field hospital. After a few days Lemm grew frustrated; simply walking out of the hospital without permission, he made his own way back to his unit. The campaign earned him the Iron Cross First Class for gallantry in action, to add to the Second Class he had received in Poland.

By the opening of Operation 'Barbarossa', OLt Lemm was commanding 2 Kompanie of I/Inf Regt 27. In September 1941 his unit were temporarily cut off behind Soviet lines; Lemm and his men held their positions against enemy attacks for two days, before breaking through to German lines bringing 50 prisoners with them. Over the winter of 1941/42, Lemm's division was one of five Army formations trapped in the Demjansk Pocket alongside the SS 'Totenkopf' Division. Initial attempts by German units outside the Pocket to break through to their 96,000 trapped comrades failed, and the encircled units had to endure a prolonged siege, depending upon the Luftwaffe for a bare minimum of supplies. On 1 April 1942, during the fighting in the Pocket, Lemm was promoted to Hauptmann. On 28 April a relief force finally broke through and held open a corridor through which the trapped divisions escaped.

Lemm's division continued to fight on the northern sector of the front, at Nevel and Vitebsk. In January 1943, Lemm was appointed to command II/Inf Regt 27; his battalion distinguished itself during a

Heinz-Georg Lemm,
photographed as a Hauptmann
and battalion commander of II/Inf
Regt 27 after the award of the
Knight's Cross on 14 April 1943.
Apart from being personally
courageous and effective, this
popular officer showed himself
to be a humane leader.

series of fierce actions, on one occasion destroying 46 Soviet tanks in three days. For his conduct in command Lemm was decorated with the Knight's Cross on 14 April 1943, being promoted to Major with effect from 1 April. In October 1943 Lemm took over the redesignated Füsilier Regt 27 pending the arrival of its new commander. He was subsequently offered a regimental command of his own, but in a new Luftwaffe Field Division; he declined, preferring to return to his own battalion. Major Lemm continued to lead them with distinction in the continuing battles on the northern Russian Front.

The month of July 1944 would bring Maj Lemm a series of shocking experiences. On 11 July he was awarded the Oak-Leaves and formally appointed commander of Füs Regt 27. As was usual, he was summoned to the Führerhauptquartier to receive the decoration from Hitler in person, and the award took place on 21 July – the day after the bomb attempt on Hitler's life. Unfortunately for Lemm, just days before he had been seen in conversation with Obst Claus von Stauffenberg, who placed the bomb. Lemm was arrested for questioning by the Gestapo, but luckily his innocence was accepted and he was soon released. As he prepared to return to his unit, however, it was overwhelmed by the massive Soviet summer offensive which smashed Army Group Centre. The 12.Inf Div found itself cut off and under orders to defend Mogilev at all costs; Soviet units were soon streaming past south of the city, and the divisional commander attempted a break-out to the north-west before it was too late. Only a small remnant succeeded in reaching the German lines on the East Prussian border, the rest of the division passing into Soviet captivity. Hitler had personally forbidden the abandonment of Mogilev, and a vindictive investigation of all senior officers of the division was only halted by the intervention of their corps commander.

The shattered 12. was rebuilt as a Volksgrenadier Division in the autumn; it achieved a strength of 14,800 men, and was unusually well equipped for that date. Many of these VG divisions were of relatively low standard, but the 12. would end the war with 24 bearers of the Knight's Cross and eight of the Oak-Leaves. Heinz-Georg Lemm was promoted to Oberstleutnant on 1 November 1944. His division served as part of I SS-Panzerkorps during the Ardennes offensive, where US intelligence rated it the best infantry division in the 6.Panzerarmee. Retreating as part of II SS-Panzerkorps, the division went into defensive positions facing the US 9th Army on the Roer river. Lemm showed his leadership qualities when, on his own initiative, he absorbed a punishment unit

Now an Oberstleutnant commanding his regiment, the 25-year-old Lemm is portrayed after being awarded the Oak-Leaves in July 1944. Note on his upper left sleeve the shield awarded to those who took part in the fighting in the Demjansk Pocket. He was also a holder of the German Cross in Gold, awarded on 19 December 1941.

into his regiment, and had all the disciplinary papers relating to the men burned, thus 'rehabilitating' them at a stroke. This greatly increased their chances of survival, since soldiers sent to such penal units were often given the most dangerous missions.

On 15 March 1945, ObstLt Lemm was decorated with the Swords in recognition of his distinguished leadership; he was also promoted to Oberst, at 25 years old the youngest to hold this rank in the German Army. When congratulated on his award and promotion, he replied, 'I would have preferred 1,000 artillery shells, or five assault guns'. In April 1945 the division was trapped in the Ruhr Pocket. Only hours before it finally surrendered, Obst Lemm was captured by US troops while leading a small reconnaissance patrol in person.

Finally released from captivity only in 1950, Lemm soon joined the new Bundeswehr of the German Federal Republic. By 1963 he held the rank of Brigadegeneral, commanding 7.PzGren Bde in 3.Pz Div; and in

1970 he was promoted Generalmajor and given command of 5.Panzer Division. Further promotion to Generalleutnant came in 1974; when he finally retired from the military in 1979, GenLt Lemm held the Grand Cross of the Federal Merit Cross with Breast Star, as well as the US Legion of Merit. Before his death in November 1994 he held the presidencies of both the Association of Knight's Cross Bearers, and the Association of German Soldiers' Organizations.

SS-Oberführer Georg Bochmann

Georg Bochmann was born on 18 September 1913 in the Saxon town of Albenau. The son of a factory worker, he enlisted in the SS-Totenkopfverbände – the SS internal security troops – in April 1934. He was commissioned SS-Untersturmführer in 1936, and posted to SS-Totenkopfstandarte I 'Oberbayern' based at Dachau. Eventually given command of 14.(Panzerjäger) Kompanie of the regiment within the new SS 'Totenkopf' Division, SS-Obersturmführer Bochmann served in the West in spring 1940. During this campaign the ill-trained and ill-equipped division suffered very heavy casualties, and some of its units earned a reputation for war crimes. With the upgrading and enlargement of 'Totenkopf' a Panzerjäger Abteilung (anti-tank battalion) had been formed, and Bochmann, now an SS-Hauptsturmführer (Captain), commanded this unit in the invasion of the USSR in 1941, when it fought on the Leningrad front.

The battalion took heavy casualties but performed much more efficiently than in 1940. (One of SS-Hstuf Bochmann's youngest soldiers, SS-Strm Fritz Christen, knocked out 13 enemy tanks while manning his gun alone, winning himself the Knight's Cross as the first enlisted man, and the youngest man, in the Waffen-SS to receive it.) Bochmann himself came to prominence during the encirclement of German forces, including the 'Totenkopf', in the Demjansk Pocket. In April 1942 Bochmann led his weary men in a successful break-out across the River Lovat and through enemy positions. They captured a number of Soviet artillery pieces in hand-to-hand fighting, during which Bochmann was seriously wounded, and reached German lines on 21 April. For this achievement Bochmann was decorated with the Knight's Cross on 3 May 1942.

The 'Totenkopf' Division had suffered more than 12,000 casualties by 20 March 1942, and by September all its combat units had recorded about 80 per cent casualties. It was withdrawn to France in October, for re-organization as the 3.SS-PzGren Div, which returned to Russia in February 1943. SS-Sturmbannführer Bochmann now commanded the mechanized infantry unit SS-PzGren Regt 5 'Thule', which saw heavy fighting under the new I SS-Panzerkorps. Bochmann was decorated with the Oak-Leaves on 17 May 1943, receiving the award personally from Hitler. He was subsequently given command of his division's SS-Pz Regt 3, and led the 'Totenkopf' tank regiment through the Kursk salient fighting of July, including the gigantic armoured clash at

SS-Sturmbannführer Georg Bochmann in seen here in field-grey service dress wearing the Knight's Cross he was awarded on 3 May 1942 as commander of the anti-tank battalion of the 'Totenkopf' Division during the defence of the Demjansk Pocket early in 1942.

Prokhorovka. Much weakened, the division saw continual fierce combat against Soviet advances around Stalino, and then in the failed defence of Kharkov in August. Throughout the autumn of 1943 the division, now one of the most trusted in the order of battle, was used as a 'fire brigade', fighting successfully but at heavy cost to stem a number of Soviet thrusts. In November 1943 it was redesignated as 3.SS-Panzer Division, and Bochmann's regiment received an increased allocation of armour.

Brought back up to strength in June 1944 after operations in Romania, the 'Totenkopf' was worn down again during desperate defensive fighting that summer in the face of the Soviet Operation 'Bagration', which forced Army Group Centre back into Poland. In August 1944, SS-Stubaf Bochmann was temporarily posted to command SS-Pz Regt 9 in the new but elite 9.SS-Pz Div 'Hohenstaufen' fighting on the Western Front. He remained in this post until January 1945, when he took command of 18.SS-Frw PzGren Div 'Horst Wessel' with the rank of SS-Oberführer. This formation was markedly inferior to his previous commands, being raised largely from ethnic German conscripts from Hungary, though it was up to strength and relatively well equipped. Thrown into battle against the Soviet armies steamrolling through Silesia, 'Horst Wessel' took a terrible mauling and was soon encircled by the Red Army near Oberglogau. As at Demjansk, Bochmann once again led a successful break-out, which saved a part of the division from certain annihilation. On 30 March 1945, SS-Oberf Bochmann was summoned to the Führerhauptquartier and decorated with the Swords. He was then given command of 17.SS-PzGren Div 'Götz von Berlichingen', a formation greatly weakened while fighting on the Western Front since June 1944. Bochmann led his new division in Bavaria and Austria for the remaining weeks of the war, only surrendering to US forces on 7 May 1945 when expressly ordered to do so by XIII Armeekorps.

Georg Bochmann died in retirement at the age of 60, and his funeral was attended by large numbers of his former soldiers.

Here SS-Stubaf Bochmann, having transferred to the command of the 'Totenkopf' Division's tank regiment, wears the special black uniform for armoured vehicle crews, again with the divisional death's-head collar patch. He displays the Oak-Leaves awarded on 17 May 1943 for his earlier command of the division's PzGren Regt 5 'Thule'.

Generalmajor Hellmuth Mäder

Hellmuth Mäder joined the Army in 1936, and by September 1939 was serving as a junior staff officer with 34.Infanterie Division. In spring 1940, Olt Mäder commanded 14 Kompanie of Inf Regt 522 in the new 297.Inf Div, which was not deployed in the Western campaign. In late 1940 he was appointed to command III Btl/Inf Regt 522, and served in that post during the opening phase of Operation 'Barbarossa'. His division fought under Army Group South, advancing on Kiev and

Bochmann receives the Oak-Leaves with Swords from Hitler at Rastenburg. Although the black Panzer uniform was only supposed to be worn on active service, many proud tank men wore it as walking-out dress and for formal occasions. Here Bochmann appears to be wearing it over a pair of officer's riding boots. (US National Archives)

Rostov, and for his gallantry during the defensive actions of winter 1941/42, Mäder was decorated with the Knight's Cross on 3 April 1942. In July 1942 he was promoted to Major and took command of Inf Regt 522, which distinguished itself during 6.Armee's drive to the Don, fighting at Kharkov, the Izyum Pocket and Voronezh.

Promoted to Oberstleutnant, Mäder led his regiment into Stalingrad, where it was cut off with the rest of 6.Armee. Hellmuth Mäder led battle groups of his regiment and others during the desperate defensive fighting of December 1942 and January 1943; fortunately for him, a serious wound led to his evacuation by air before the final collapse, in which his regiment and division were destroyed. On recovering from his wounds Mäder was placed on the so-called Führerreserve until early 1944.

Mäder as Generalmajor and commander of the elite Führer Grenadier Division. Note the unusual combination of uniform items: the field-grey 'cross-over' jacket authorized for self-propelled artillery and tank destroyer crews, with general officer's collar patches added, and red-striped general officer's breeches with riding boots.

Promoted to Oberst, he was given command of the so-called Eingreifbrigade Narwa and returned to the northern sector of the Eastern Front. Here he was successful in halting a number of localized Soviet attacks before being seriously wounded once again. This time, on recovery from his wounds he was appointed commander of Heeresgruppen Waffenschule Nord, a weapons training establishment. This respite was brief, however: when the Soviets launched their great 1944 summer offensives he returned to the front, being given responsibility for organizing the defence of a vital railway junction at Schaulen, between Königsberg and Riga. He held it open under heavy attack for two days, allowing retreating German units to pass safely through. For this achievement he was awarded the Oak-Leaves on 27 August 1944.

That autumn Mäder served briefly as deputy commander of 7.Pz Div, again on the north Russian Front; and at the end of 1944 he was given command of the elite Führer Begleit Brigade, a part of Panzerkorps 'Grossdeutschland'. He led it through the ill-fated Ardennes offensive, and when, early in 1945, the brigade was expanded to become the Führer Grenadier Division, the promoted GenMaj Mäder was its commander. The new division saw fierce fighting on the Eastern Front near Stettin, before being forced to retreat south-west to the approaches of Vienna. Here, during the final battles for the Austrian capital, GenMaj Mäder was awarded the Swords on 18 April 1945. The division surrendered to US forces three weeks later. Although Mäder had surrendered to the Americans, he was handed over to the Soviets, who held him in captivity until late 1955.

Mäder subsequently joined the Bundeswehr, serving with the rank of Brigadegeneral and in 1956 receiving command of the Infanterieschule at Hammelburg. He was promoted to Generalleutnant in 1969, finally retiring in 1974.

Oberst Hellmuth Mäder is seen here wearing the Oak-Leaves he received in August 1944; during the Soviet advances of that summer he was given operational command of the strategic town of Schaulen in Lithuania, and defended it effectively.

SS-Sturmbannführer Otto Weidinger

Born in Würzburg on 27 May 1914, Otto Weidinger volunteered for the SS-Verfügungstruppe in April 1934; he entered the SS-Junkerschule at Braunschweig in May 1935 and was commissioned as an SS-Unter-sturmführer in April 1936. His first command was 3 Kompanie of SS-Standarte 'Deutschland' at Ellwangen. Shortly afterwards he undertook a course for combat engineers with the SS-Pioniere Bataillon, as well as attending the Kampfschule at Au.

After promotion to SS-Obersturmführer in September 1938 he was temporarily attached to the Army; on returning to his regiment he served as adjutant in both the motorcycle battalion and later the reconnaissance unit. In November 1939, Weidinger was appointed to command the armoured car company of this Aufklärungs Abteilung, and earned the Iron Cross Second Class in this role during the Polish campaign, when two SS-VT regiments acquitted themselves well while attached to Army Group Kempf.

In the June 1940 campaign the regiments of the new SS-Verfügungs Division were heavily engaged in both Holland and France, and Weidinger won the Iron Cross First Class before being transferred to the divisional staff. Promoted to SS-Hauptsturmführer (Captain) in July, he was appointed as divisional adjutant. He served in the Balkans the following spring; and in the early stages of the invasion of the USSR he commanded the heavy motorcycle company of the newly renamed 'Reich' Division's reconnaissance battalion. He was then posted as an instructor to the SS-Junkerschule at Braunschweig, subsequently being promoted SS-Sturmbannführer (Major).

In June 1943, SS-Stubaf Weidinger returned to the front and was given command of I Btl, SS-PzGren Regt 3 'Deutschland' in what was

SS-Stubaf Günther Wisliceny (1912–85) as commander of III/PzGren Regt 3 'Deutschland' of 2.SS-Pz Div 'Das Reich'. Wisliceny wears the metal death's-head from a service cap pinned to an Army officer's field cap; and note the lack of silver cord edging to his collar patches – a variation occasionally seen on field uniforms. Wisliceny's career closely paralleled that of Otto Weidinger of the same division. Enlisting in the SS-Stabswache Berlin in 1933, he was posted in 1938 to the 'Der Führer' Regt, seeing his first action as a company commander in the Balkans in spring 1941. He spent 1941–43 on the Eastern Front and 1944 in France, fighting in all the great actions of the senior SS divisions, and being wounded four times. He was awarded the Knight's Cross for leadership of a battalion during the battles for the Kursk salient in July 1943; the Oak-Leaves on 26 December 1944, for the Normandy campaign; and the Swords on 6 May 1945, for the final battles in the Ardennes, Hungary and Austria. In 1945 he was handed over by the US Army to the French during investigations into his division's war crimes at Tulle and Oradour, but was released in 1951.

Wisliceny with his regimental commander, SS-Staf Heinz Harmel, whom he would later succeed in command when the latter was promoted to lead 10.-SS-Pz Div 'Frundsberg' in May 1944.

now SS-PzGren Div 'Das Reich'. In this elite formation he took part in
the battle for the Kursk salient in July; Weidinger was seriously wounded
in the lung, and his unit suffered heavy casualties. During the relentless
Red Army advances that followed the failure of the Kursk offensive,
Weidinger and his men fought in many defensive actions and
counter-attacks. Often involved in close combat himself, Weidinger was
wounded once again, this time by grenade fragments. On 26 November
1943 he received the German Cross in Gold for distinguished leadership
and personal gallantry.

At the end of 1943 the 'Das Reich' was withdrawn to Germany to be re-organized and re-equipped as the 2.SS-Pz Div; however, the situation at the front required that an armoured battle group – SS-Pz Kampfgruppe 'Das Reich' – remain on the Eastern Front. Otto Weidinger served with it, now in command of a composite Panzergrenadier regiment bearing the divisional title. Weidinger's regiment took part in the battle for the Cherkassy Pocket, fighting in the rearguard. In April 1944 the bulk of the Kampfgruppe rejoined the parent division in France; but once again, Weidinger was to remain in Russia, now with a much reduced battle group which saw fierce combat around Tarnopol. He earned the personal Close Combat Clasp; and on 21 April 1944 he was decorated with the Knights Cross.

A few weeks later, on 14 June 1944, SS-Stubaf Weidinger was given command of the division's SS-PzGren Regt 4 'Der Führer', now on the Western Front. This unit was committed to fierce fighting against US troops near St Lô and eventually became encircled near Coutances; after breaking out, the survivors were thrown into the hopeless counter-attack at Mortain. Although it suffered heavy casualties, 'Das Reich' succeeded in escaping the final destruction of the German forces in the Falaise Pocket, crossing the Seine to temporary safety at the end of August.

In December 1944 the division, including Weidinger's 'Der Führer' Regt, took part in the Ardennes offensive as part of 6.SS-Panzerarmee. Initially held in reserve, the regiment was eventually committed to battle on 19 December, taking part in the attack on St Vith. Weidinger's troops had come close to reaching the Meuse when the weather finally cleared and allowed the Allies to make use of their overwhelming air power. The regiment suffered heavy casualties during the American counter-attacks;

SS-Panzergrenadiers of the 'Das Reich' Division, supported by a StuG III self-propelled assault gun, on the steppes east of Kiev in early September 1943, after the final loss of Kharkov in the fourth battle for that city. (Private collection)

and on 28 December 1944, SS-Stubaf Weidinger was awarded the
Oak-Leaves for leadership in both Normandy and the Ardennes.

In early March 1945, the 'Das Reich' was committed to Operation
'Spring Awakening' near Lake Balaton in Hungary, 6.SS-Panzerarmee's
vain attempt to retake Budapest and vital oilfields. When the attempt
bogged down in the mud the advancing Red Army pushed the division
westward into Austria, where it took part in the defence of Vienna in
April. The 'Der Führer' Regt was sent to Czechoslovakia, where it
helped suppress the insurrection in Prague before moving westwards
and surrendering to US forces west of Pilsen on 9 May 1945. Just three
days before, on 6 May, Otto Weidinger had been awarded the Swords.

After the war Weidinger wrote the definitive combat history of his
division, and was the president of the divisional veterans' organization.

THE PLATES

A: THE KNIGHT'S CROSS AND OAK-LEAVES WITH SWORDS, AWARD DOCUMENT & CASE

1 The Knight's Cross and Oak-Leaves with Swords attached – an example of the clasp by Steinhauer und Lück of Lüdenscheid. Note the difference in shape and size of the Swords when compared with the formal award piece (**2**). The Steinhauer swords are also plain on the reverse. This firm were never given an official contract to supply these to the government, and any encountered must be considered as made for the retail market or as display pieces for museums, military outfitters' shops, etc.

2 A fine example of a standard award clasp by Godet of Berlin. The speckled effect is natural age tarnish; when new the clasps were finished in a matt white silver oxide effect with burnished highlights. The reverse shows the silver content '900' to the left and the maker's contract code '21' to the right. Note that the Swords are detailed on both sides; and that the ribbon suspension loop is longer than that for the basic Oak-Leaves. (Courtesy Jason Burmeister Collection)

3 An example of the formal award document for the Oak-Leaves with Swords. The exterior of the folder (left) has a gilt metallic eagle-and-swastika and geometric bordering attached to the white leather facing; 'page 3' of the folded parchment (right) was hand-lettered in red-brown ink calligraphy with the national emblem and the recipient's name hand-tooled in gold leaf. The example shown here – to General Rommel – has been completed by the studio team and is ready for Hitler's signature. It was featured in the period publication *Kunst im dritten Reich* ('Art in the Third Reich'), which confirms the perceived status as this *Urkunde* as a work of art.

B: 'PAPA' HOTH AT KURSK, JULY 1943

An example of an officer awarded the higher grades of the Knight's Cross for his command performance rather than acts of individual bravery, General Hermann Hoth – commanding the armoured spearhead of Army Group South during Operation 'Citadel' – is seen in a battlefield conference with officers of his staff during the huge operations against the Kursk salient. He wears a relatively austere uniform, including the *Feldmütze* with gold general officer's piping and insignia but apparently retaining the 'V' in arm-of-service colour, here the rose-pink of Panzer troops. His general's field-grey tunic, with the usual officers' green collar facing, bears the gold bullion wire *'alt Larisch'* insignia of general rank on scarlet patches, and the shoulder boards of full general; his breast eagle is embroidered in gold bullion on black Panzer backing. The only decoration Hoth displayed was his Knight's Cross with Oak-Leaves. His stone-grey breeches have the general officer's scarlet *Lampassen* – two broad stripes flanking seam piping. In the background, the SdKfz 250/3 radio half-track which he is using as a command vehicle has been temporarily fitted with

A group of Waffen-SS officers receive their Oak-Leaves with Swords from Hitler at the Führerhauptquartier. At far left, the Walloon volunteer commander Leon Degrelle; in the background, behind Herbert-Otto Gille, stands Hermann Fegelein. (US National Archives)

the gold-on-grey pennant of a general officer on the right mudguard and the square flag of an army commander on the right. The staff officers are reconstructed as an Army artillery Major, and an SS-Obersturmbannführer of SS-Panzer Regiment 3 'Totenkopf'.

C: HERMANN FEGELEIN HUNTING PARTISANS, JUNE 1943

This officer represents a rather less respectable example of a 'command' award of the higher grades of the Knight's Cross, almost certainly due to his status as a favourite of Reichsführer-SS Heinrich Himmler. In May–July 1943, SS-Brigadeführer Fegelein's 8.SS-Kavallerie Division 'Florian Geyer' was engaged in 'anti-partisan operations' in its old 1941 haunts between the Dnieper river and the Pripet Marshes of central Russia; such sweeps did involve combat against large armed bands, but also widespread atrocities against civilian villagers. Conferring over maps spread on the bonnet of a Kubelwagen, MajGen Fegelein presents, as always, a rather dandified figure. His headgear is an SS service cap with the chin cords and buttons removed, cavalry-yellow piping, and a woven Army national insignia above the SS death's-head on the black velvet band. Over cavalry officer's service uniform he wears a privately

acquired field jacket tailored to the same cut as his white summer undress tunic, but in camouflage cloth from a Waffen-SS *Zeltbahn* tent sheet. It bears no insignia or decorations apart from his Knight's Cross with Oak-Leaves. Fegelein carries his habitual riding whip. The other figures are his younger brother Waldemar, then an SS-Sturmann-führer commanding the division's SS-Kavallerie Regiment 2; and a senior NCO of his division, reporting after a reconnaissance patrol. The so-called 'palm-tree' pattern SS camouflage smock was wisely used in the cavalry formation. Obsolescent weapons, like the Erm MPE, were still seen in use with SS anti-partisan units.

D: FRANZ BÄKE IN THE BALABANOVKA POCKET, JANUARY 1944

During defensive fighting in the Oratoff area of the southern Ukraine in late January–early February 1944, Oberstleutnant Bäke, commander of Panzer Regiment 11 from 6.Panzer Division, led a battlegroup consisting of his own I Bataillon equipped with PzKw V Panthers, the PzKw VI Tigers of schwere Panzer Abteilung 503, and some self-propelled assault guns. In one five-day period the Kampfgruppe destroyed 267 Soviet armoured vehicles, for the loss of only one Tiger and four Panthers. Here LtCol Bäke has left his own vehicle to give personal orders to an NCO commanding Tiger '221', a battered tank of 2.Kompanie/sPzAbt 503 (of which a photo from this period survives). Both men wear standard black Panzer vehicle uniform; one photo shows Bäke wearing over this the Army's padded reversible winter combat jacket.

E: 'GERD' BARKHORN'S 250TH VICTORY, 13 FEBRUARY 1944

A photo recorded Hptm Barkhorn's welcome at an airstrip south of Kiev on the day he became only the second pilot to achieve 250 'kills', for which he would be decorated with the Swords at Berchtesgaden a few weeks later. (He travelled part of the way with fellow aces Erich Hartmann, Walter Krupinski and Johannes Wiese, who were all to receive the Oakleaves; the young fighter pilots drank far too much, and Hitler's staff were terrified that they would misbehave during the ceremony.) The Gruppenkommandeur of II/JG 52 had achieved his most recent 50 victories in just 75 days. Sharing a toast with his ground crew chief, Barkhorn wears a suitably 'softened' Luftwaffe officer's service cap, and the sheepskin-lined KW Fl bR/41 two-piece flying suit with electrical connectors for heated gloves and boots. Barkhorn flew several different Bf 109G-6 fighters, with slight variations to the Gruppenkomandeur's double chevron marking (see Osprey, Aircraft of the Aces 37, *Bf 109 Aces of the Russian Front*), but constants were his wife's name 'Christl' under the cockpit, and a small white '5'.

F: 'FIPS' PHILIPP OF THE 'GREEN HEARTS', MARCH 1942

Hauptmann Hans Philipp, appointed Gruppenkommandeur of I/JG 54 on 14 February 1942, was awarded the Swords on 12 March on achieving his 82nd 'kill'; on the 31st of that month he became only the fourth fighter pilot in the Luftwaffe to reach 100 aerial victories. Although the Soviet winter counter-offensive of 1941/42 had inflicted a brutal check on the Wehrmacht, the Red Air Force was still notably inferior to

An informal study of Gerhard Barkhorn (Plate E), dressed in typical fighter pilot's garb of fur-collared winter flying jacket and service cap. The Knight's Cross was worn at all times, even in combat.

the Luftwaffe in both equipment and skill, and Jagdgeschwader 54 'Grünherz' continued to run up an impressive score of victories. Based at Siverskaya on the Leningrad front in north Russia, JG 54 collectively recorded 201 kills during February alone, for the loss of just 18 Messerschmitt Bf 109s; and by 4 April the Geschwader would achieve their 2,000th victory of the war. Hans Philipp's Bf 109F-2 illustrated here shows a rudder tally of 87 kills. It bears the tactical marking of a Staff Major, despite his status as Gruppenkommandeur; the Geschwader badge was painted below the cockpit, and that of I Gruppe on the cowling. The yellow areas under the nose and wingtips and the yellow fuselage band were standard quick recognition devices for German aircraft in Russia. A portrait photo shows Philipp holding a pet fox cub. He wears the usual Luftwaffe 'flight blouse', here with the sheepskin-lined trousers of the KW Fl bR/41 flying suit and issue flying boots.

G: ERICH RUDORFFER IN KARELIA, JUNE 1944

In the first months of 1944 the Soviet offensive on the Leningrad front saw the two Fw 190-equipped Gruppen of JG 54 'Grünherz' rushed back from the central and southern sectors to their old hunting grounds in north Russia. In June the Red Army unleashed their massive Operation 'Bagration' against Army Group Centre to the south, threatening to cut off the German and Finnish armies in Courland and the Karelian peninsula respectively. Shortly after being awarded the Oak-Leaves, Major Rudorffer led his II Gruppe to Immola in Finland to provide fighter cover for Stukas and ground-attack Focke-Wulfs gathered in a temporary battle group, Gefechtsverband Kuhlmey. During their month at Immola his group would claim 66 Soviet aircraft shot down. Rudorffer's Fw 190A-6 did not at this date bear the Geschwader's usual 'Green Heart' insignia; and his low-visibility Gruppenkommandeur's double chevrons displayed a small additional black '1'. In 1943 and 1944 many aircraft of I and II/JG 54 had the bottom part of their rudder painted yellow (see Osprey, Aircraft of the Aces 6, *Focke-Wulf Fw 190 Aces of the Russian Front*). A photo of Rudorffer shows him wearing the standard summer two-piece K So/41 flying suit; the thousands of lakes in Finland also made it sensible to wear the SWp 10-30 B2 inflatable life vest.

H: OTTO WEIDINGER AT THE FLORISDORFER BRIDGE, 9 APRIL 1945

In the first week of April 1945 the remnants of 2.SS-Panzer Division 'Das Reich' – driven back out of Hungary following the failure of 6.SS-Panzerarmee's abortive Operation 'Spring Awakening' the previous month – were fighting in the streets of Vienna. This painting is based on a snapshot taken on about 9 April near the Florisdorfer Bridge, where mechanized infantry from LtCol Weidinger's SS-Panzergrenadier Regiment 4 'Der Führer' were attempting to hold the Danube crossings against the advancing Red Army (coincidentally, the regiment had originally been raised in Austria, and based at Graz). Several photographs taken during these actions show the tired and battle-worn Weidinger visiting his units riding a solo motorcycle, dressed in the loosely cut Army motorcyclist's coat of rubberized cloth with wool collar facing, a steel helmet with a Waffen-SS camouflage cover, and gauntlet mittens. He displays the Knight's Cross with

Oak-Leaves at the throat of his tunic; the standard SS-rune and Obersturmbannführer's rank patches on his collar; and shoulder boards attached to the coat, showing his rank and the gilt 'DF' cypher of his regiment.

SS-Ostubaf Otto Weidinger (Plate H) photographed in April 1945 near the Florisdorfer Bridge, Vienna.

INDEX